PENGUIN BOOKS

GREAT POP THINGS

COLIN B. MORTON was born on 6/6/60 up Twm Barlwn, GWENT CITY WALES, his starsign is NONE and he was Educated at Bristol Poly studying "Ideologies and Utopia" under Clive Barker

REAL NAME: clark Gwent

FAVE Record: Trout Mask REPLICA (of course.)

FAVE Rave By Dave: "letter to hermygnome"

motto: "A foolish consistency is the laughing gnome of little minds"

Favourite cartoonist: Rene Magritte

Favourite Actor: Donald Pleasance, **Actress:** Christina Ricci

Chuck Ulysses D'Eath was born in a US. missile base in Caerwent on April first 1966 of Welsh/Winnebego Sioux parentage. Expelled from Leeds University for doing cartoons chuck's favourite drink is Duke of Clarence, Rich Malmsey wine AND Tetleys. **Punchline to Favorite Joke:** ...."Because it's his NEWT!..." HA HA!

Fashion Guru: Elvis Aaaron Presley

Regrets: "I will probably never read the news for the BBC"

Chuck and Colin's other strip-creations have included HECATE, which chronicled the adventures of the world's 1st transvestite super-hero, and THE BORING WORLD OF SNAILS which chronicled the adventures of some snails. They are currently rehearsing RAIN PUDDING, their (Suicide/Pet shop Boys inspired) band for a tour and LP, working on a (spinal Tap meets the Commitments in 'Post Punk UK) film script called the REZEMBLERS and a SCI-FI graphic novel combining the Elvis/Jesus/Superman legends- "Junk Mail of the Gods."

"...one night I had a dream, in which Bob Dylan came to my house and we went down the pub. I wanted to impress my friends with my new aquaintance, but they just said "hi Bob" and he said 'hi' back to them ....on the same night Chuck had a similar dream except when he and Mr. Dylan got to the pub, chuck couldn't find anyone he knew...this in essence, sums up the difference between chuck and myself....."

Colin B. Morton 1992

COLIN B.

"...I saw Dave Bowie recently. I was walking behind these three girls over the footbridge at Newport station. One of them said,'LOOK THERE'S DAVE...' and ran over to him. Throwing her arms around his neck, she said 'DAVID, IT'S BEEN SUCH A LONG TIME...' I had this terrible urge to go up and draw a zig-zag on his head..."

chuck Death 1992

chuck and Colin would like to dedicate this book to the people of GWENT in honour of their invention: PUNK ROCK - Also thanks to Eleanor Levy, RJ Smith sue Cummings and the rough tongued hunks at NME

CHUCK

COLIN B. MORTON AND CHUCK DEATH

GREAT POP THINGS

WITH AN INTRODUCTION
BY GREIL MARCUS

PENGUIN BOOKS

PENGUIN BOOKS

Published by the Penguin Group
Penguin Books Ltd, 27 Wrights Lane, London W8 5TZ, England
Penguin Books USA Inc., 375 Hudson Street, New York, New York 10014, USA
Penguin Books Australia Ltd, Ringwood, Victoria, Australia
Penguin Books Canada Ltd, 10 Alcorn Avenue, Toronto, Ontario, Canada M4V 3B2
Penguin Books (NZ) Ltd, 182–190 Wairau Road, Auckland 10, New Zealand

Penguin Books Ltd, Registered Offices: Harmondsworth, Middlesex, England

The cartoons in this book were first published in *New Musical Express*, *L. A. Weekly*
and *Record Mirror*
This collection published in Penguin Books 1992
1 3 5 7 9 10 8 6 4 2

Printed in England by Clays Ltd, St Ives plc

INTRODUCTION

by Greil Marcus

Recently one Philip Tagg, a musicologist, published a 150-page analysis of Abba's "Fernando". ("It's not even their best song," a reviewer remarked.) Not long before, a particularly addled scholar devoted 500 pages to unraveling the supposed mysteries of the Sex Pistols' "Anarchy in the U.K.".

With these and other absurdities upon us, it is plain a completely new approach to pop criticism and pop history is needed. Of course, the indelible contributions pop performers have made to the occasionally dicey survival of Western civilization must be acknowledged – but also the fact that the very same performers can instantly rise to levels of cretinism so irritating that were the end of Western civilization the price of their disappearance, it would hardly be held too dear. Coincidentally, this is exactly the approach taken in the pages that follow by comix artists Colin B. Morton and Chuck Death.

Here, all of pop history is turned into one grand and interlocking pun, with inside dope, fans' legends, and actual truth smeared until even the significant is a moment of the trivial, and vice versa. The pop past is not merely retold, it is corrected: if once an outraged folkie screamed, "JUDAS!" at Bob Dylan and his new electric guitar, now a less apocalyptic "BOO! Do you know any Judas Priest?" seems infinitely more telling. The responsibilities of pop sociology are not ignored, just twisted. Punk rockers, we are told, "wore ridiculous outfits, didn't have proper jobs and said beastly things about the Royal Family (who also wore ridiculous clothes and didn't have proper jobs)"; in installment number 3 of the Adam Ant Story there is an instructive lecture on why money *does* grow on trees. One meets familiar figures: the Devil (rendezvousing with Vanilla Ice at the crossroads to teach him how to rap, or making off with the souls of Led Zeppelin, save that of skeptical bass player Jean-Paul Sartre – "Non," he demurs, "l'occultisme, c'est un grand sac de merde"), "Pacifist Philosopher Louis Fakkarakkaran", the Kray Twins (surrendering to the police rather than take on Sid Vicious), a former Prime Minister, affectionately remembered ("Margaret Hecate Thatcher, Whore of Babylon"), and even Jesus Himself ("the first punk rocker", a priest insists). In the blank eyes of Bros, one is transported right back into *The Village of the Damned*.

The panels themselves are busy, jammed with references bumping into each other and into those of strips ten or twenty pages before or after. Very little, in these versions of the pop faces that have been reproduced so many millions of times over, is precisely what it seems. Sometimes it is, though – as with one signal drawing of Johnny Rotten, who first appears as a tubercular waif in a Hogarthian re-creation of that famous day when he was kidnapped by a child molester in front of Malcolm McLaren's SEX shop (sorry, I mean recruited for a pop group), and takes on final form only much later.

In full regalia, dripping badges, strips of clothing, and a huge safety pin, his mouth opens. "GO AWAY I DON'T LIKE ANY OF YOU, MAAAN!" he says – and he looks just like a compost pile. I cut that panel out of the paper when it first appeared, a couple of years ago, and pinned it to the wall. I look at it every week or so, always wondering: *How does it feel to get something so right?* That is one of the few pop questions not answered in *Great Pop Things*.

GREAT POP THINGS → THE DAWN OF ROCK BY COLIN B. MORTON & CHUCK DEATH

The early 1950's everywhere were really boring. Teenagers had nothing to do but watch T.V., which in those days consisted of a test card, a woman called Muriel and a windmill going around and around and around and around....

But soon the youth of the world were caught on fire by ROCK 'N' ROLL!!! Bill Haley was the first white man to invent Rock 'n' roll, unfortunately he was a small, chubby man who wasn't very good at it. Bill became the only rock singer to die of old age..............

The second white man to invent rock'n'roll was ELVIS PRESLEY. He sung like a black man. Previously there had been Sammy Davis Junior, a black man who sung like a white man, but that, like Bill Haley, didn't really catch on.......

Elvis became very famous indeed, despite upsetting many establishment figures such as FRANKIE SINATRA who was a bit cross because his mate Sammy Davis Junior had got it the wrong way around.............. THE END.

GREAT POP THINGS → DAVE BOWIE: "the Chameleon of Rock" Part one. by Colin B. Morton & Chuck Death

Dave Bowie was born in Brixton, London, in 1947, under the assumed name of "David Jones." This was the first inkling that he was to become **THE CHAMELEON OF ROCK!!**

From the very start he was not like other people. At school Dave frequently got into trouble for cutting up library books and using the wrong changing-rooms.

After leaving school Dave became part of the "burgeoning "MOD" movement. His single "**I'M A LAUGHING GNOME**" became an anthem for the young "mods"...

It is a little known fact that Dave tried to join the MONKEES but was rejected because they already had an English person called Dave Jones and didn't want any more.

GREAT POP THINGS → DAVE BOWIE "the chameleon of ROCK" PART 2   BY Colin B. Morton & Chuck DEATH

Disheartened at his rejection from the MONKEES (see part 1) Dave enrolled in the Lindsey Kamp Mime school. Here he learnt useful skills such as pretending he was in a box that was getting smaller and smaller and...

Another great influence on Dave was the "cut-out" poems of Mr. William Burroughs. This means cutting up old newspapers and putting them back together to make a song.... (SEE EXAMPLE ABOVE)

Two of Dave's most outstanding characteristics are "bending" and an obsession with "insanity"... It is a little known fact that Dave has a brother, Terry Jones, who hasn't got all his chairs in the house. Terry has often appeared in public in "Drag" or screaming in a high pitched voice.

It is one of Dave's greatest fears that he too has a kangaroo loose in his top paddock, thus the twin spectres of loopiness and "bending" have frequently loomed large in Dave's oeuvre, in such songs as "Aled Insane" or the film "Lavyrinth" where Dave has hair like a girlie!!!!

GREAT POP THINGS → DAVE BOWIE "the chameleon of Rock" PART 3   BY COLIN B MORTON and Chuck DEATH

Throughout the years Dave was to "act" in many, diverse roles in many and varied great films. In the "STARMAN who fell to earth" he played an androgynous and distant alien being.........

In HAPPY BIRTHDAY, LAWRENCE OF ARABIA he played a distant androgynous prisoner of war. In THE HUNGER he played an androgynous and distant vampire as well as a distant androgynous elephant in the Broadway hit ELEPHANT MAN!

Probably the most controversial time in Dave's career was when he flirted with the NAZIs in the mid-70's. Nazis were big, blonde, blue-eyed chaps who didn't like "bending" and were invented by ADOLF HITLER. Dave later apologised to shocked commuters saying he was "only trying to stop a train"..........

Despite his assertion that "WHAT BRITAIN NEEDS IS A RIGHT WING DICTATORSHIP" Dave moved to live in SWITZERLAND after Margaret Thatcher became Queen of England in 1979, thus proving once more that he is the CHAMELEON OF ROCK!

The Banananas first record was "Amma Waeei Waeee Woo" which was not a big hit despite its obvious commercial potential and catchy title. However, they attracted the attention of the ironically named Funbottom 3 who had split from the SPECIALS due to the lack of ska revivals.

"It ain't no good the way you do it" was their 'joint' hit. This started the vogue for remakes of 50's hits done with techno scratty beats plus woos woos which was to piss everybody off become extremely popular in the late 80's and early 90's yawn zzzzzzzzz................

BANANANAANA soon became famous for their fantastic singing & dancing ability plus their big 12 inch hits, although eventually all the going "woo-woo" took its toll on BAN-ANANAANA and the inevitable musical differences, inevitably occurred ....

The blonde one that everyone fancied said she wanted to give the fans something different and she dyed her hair black in order to get back to her roots. So they kicked her out and got a new dark-haired girlie in instead...... (TO BE CONTINUED)

To show there was no hard feelings, BANANANA recorded "BANANANA BANANANA HEY HEY HEY GOOD BYE EYE" as a kind of tribute to the blonde one who had left, dyed her hair black, got married to D. Stuart out of the Arythmics and went on to form a brilliant group called MORRISEY'S SISTER OF MERCY...

The highlight of BANANANAANA's career was when French and Sanders included them in a "Comic RELIEF" sketch in which they all pretended to be in a fantastic all singing, all dancing top girlie group called BANAANANAANA!!...

In 1989 they rose as high as the TOP40 with their new record "SYMPATHY FOR THE DEVIL WITH EVERYTHING BUT THE WOO-WOOS TAKEN OUT", which followed hot on the heels of "SYMPATHY FOR THE DEVIL WITH EVERYTHING BUT THE INSTRUMENTAL TRACK TAKEN OUT" by Spinal Scream...

Banananaana became the most popular girlie group ever in the history of the world, when with their 1,000,009th single they finally sold more singles than the Supremes did in their entire 23 single run. THEY HEY HEY ALL LIVED HAPPILY EVER AFTER!... THE END.

GREAT POP THINGS → DO IT YOURSELF PAUL SIMON KIT by Colin B. Morton & Chuck Death

Enclosed: 1 x lifesize cut-out Paul Simon, 1 x easy to understand "Rhymin' Simon" lyric kit containing all those oh-so-important Paul Simon type words e.g. "DOUBT", "BOY", "HAZY" and most importantly "shoes". One map of the third world and a selection of romantic, exotic ethnic LP sleeves to glue your cut-out Paul Simon onto! YES! now you too can be Paul Simon in the piracy......oops we mean privacy of your own home (offer available in USA and EEC only!!!)

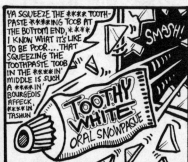

DID YOU KNOW THAT AN AXLOTYL IS A LIZARD........

Guns and f***ing Roses had very strict views on chemical abuse and would often sack other members of the band or even themselves until they didn't know whether they were coming or going.................

Waxl would also get into fights with other pop groups, tossing down his black leather gauntlet and challenging them to fisticuffs at dawn. Unfortunately he tried this with Babes in Toyland and got a good kicking....

Slasher, the "lead guitarist" of Guns and f***ing Roses is famous for being the easiest person to draw cartoons of in the world and bases his image on Cousin IT from the Addams Family and Keef Richard...

The other members of Guns and Roses are not really famous for anything interesting apart from playing their instruments quite well, although Izzy Stradling-Thomas once got thrown out of a plane for urinating in a matchbox...

The music of Guns and f***ing Roses is an amalgam of Heavy Metal and seminal British punk like the Sex Pistols and the Mekons. They have got in trouble for their lyrics which attack establishment figures such as gays and immigrants........

Their lyrics have become so notorious that they are even studied by high-brow "intellectuals" in special seminars at U.C.L.A. and Yale. Students search for underlying metaphors & what the hell he's on about.......

Guns and Roses embody the true rebellious nature of rock 'n' roll and get in trouble for doing dangerous things like pinching cameras and saying f*** in Wembley stadium (breaking the "no swearing in England" rule which has been in force since the 1970's).....

Guns and Roses articulate the inarticulacy of a generation. They speak for those kids called Jeff and Kelly who hang out in shopping malls drinking cheap soda and chewing on styrofoam containers...... THE END

......THAT NEVER REACHES IT'S MATURE STATE?

GREAT POP THINGS → THE CLASH: THEY TRIED TO CHANGE THE WORLD WITH THEIR SHORT HAIR AND TROUSERS WITH WORDS ON THEM! BY CHUCK DEATH & COLIN!

one day, when Joe Strummer, then of the 101'ers was walking along Portobello Rd, Brixton, he was approached by Mick Jones and Paul Simononon who asked him to join →THE CLASH!!!!!

they were managed by Bernie Rhodes, who moulded their image..... suggesting for instance that they wear trousers with words on them. This would make them stand apart from other groups of their day, (AEROSMITH, WOMBLES) who did not wear trousers with words on them.......

they also differed from such groups by singing about events from their everyday lives, e.g. "Pigeons on the roof" which was about a policeman taking some air rifles off them, "GarageLand" about old ladies complaining about them practising too loudly and "Career Opportunities" about how none of them could get proper jobs.........

In the name of socialism, they tried to put as many L.P.s into one sleeve as possible. While "The Clash" had only one record in it, "London Calling" had two for the same price! When "SANDINISTA" came out with three L.P.s in it for the same price, the record company noticed and told them to "CUT THE CRAP"; hence the title of their final L.P. (which only had one in it!)

GREAT POP THINGS → THE CLASH: Part Two "BUSKING into OBLIVION" By Colin B. Morton & Chuck DEATH

When MICK JONES left to form BIG BAD DYNAMITE and "TIPPER" Headon was arrested for holding up a bus-stop, Joe and Paul Simon decided to form a new look Clash consisting of them and three other blokes who nobody know who they were......

Due to their failure to make any cash outside pubs in Leeds the CLASH finally split up in 1986. Mick is still in BAD AUDIO COMPANY, Paul Simononon is in a group in L.A. who nobody knows who they are. Nobody knows what happened to the other three blokes (who nobody knew who they were)

One day, when Joe Strummer was coming out of the GEORGE ROPEY pub in London's little Belfast he was approached by Shane McGUIGAN who asked him to join the traditional Irish drunk-rock band THE POGIES for a wee while..........................

But it was in the GLITZY world of showbiz and the SILVER SCREEN that Joe was to make his mark, winning an OSCAR nomination for his role as "the man 'oo never had nuffink'" in Alex ROEG's spaghetti western "Straight to HELL" (which was coincidentally a song by the clash!) THE END

GREAT POP THINGS → The MORRISSEY STORY Part 1 "THE SMITHS STORY" BY COLIN B. MORTON AND CHUCK DEATH

Steven Morrissey was born in Manchester, Yorkshire and for the first 24 years of his life he stayed in his bedroom and didn't ever speak to ANYONE!!!.......

Occasionally he would go out for walks in the graveyard to cheer himself up. One day he met a girl called Linder who also liked graveyards and they became chums.

As it happened, Manchester became the third place in Britain to be shaken by the wild and exciting "**PUNK ROCK FEVER**" (after Newport, Gwent and London.....)

One day progressive Rock fan John Marr asked Linder if she knew anyone who could write words. So Johnny went down the dark cobbled alley to Steven's cottage...

GREAT POP THINGS → "Those CHARMING SMITHS": the MORRISSEY STORY Part 2 BY Colin B. Morton & CHUCK DEATH.

Johnny Marr asked Morrissey to read some of his lyrics to see if they were any use. Morrissey got out an old dog-eyed school exercise book and began to sing in the trembling manner which has now become familiar to millions of teens across the world.........

The SMITHS were named after Dr. Zachary Smith from TV's "LOST IN SPACE", who was Morrissey's hero due to the fact that he would run and hide whenever a monster attacked, thereby subverting conventional notions of male sexuality.........

The Smiths were a big big success, and sold millions of their independent records. But despite all the pressure of their stardom morrissey stayed true to his heroes Kenneth Williams & Charles Hawtrey and never did sex with anybody ever...................

But all did not go smoothly and they got fired by Rough Records for pretending Queen Elizabeth II had died. The Smiths split up so Johnny Marr could reform the Beatles and morrissey could complete a 3 month prison sentence for treason. THE END

GREAT POP THINGS → The BEACH BOYS STORY By Colin B. Morton and Chuck Death

In the early 60's the "surf" craze started: this consisted of youths paddling out to sea with a piece of wood, jumping on it, and then floating back to the shore.....

Unlike previous youth crazes (e.g. the Hula Hoop) a genre of music sprung up to accompany "surfing." It's primary exponents were THE BEACH BOYS!..

One of the BEACH BOYS, Brian later went crackers and tried to make perfect pop records by playing a grand piano full of sand (ONLY DENIS BEACH ACTUALLY SURFED AND HE DIED IN A SWIMMING POOL.

The rest of the BEACH BOYS carried on without him. They are still going today. Although no longer "boys", they decided to keep it on the name because the "The Beach" doesn't sound very good. THE END.

GREAT POP THINGS → The FALL Story - THEY TRIED TO CHANGE THE WORLD WITH THEIR PROLE ART THREATS AND STUFF — BY Colin B. Morton & Chuck Death.

Mark Egbert Smith was born in Manchester, Derbyshire. As a child he was not like other children as he often saw ghosts all over the place. When punk rock shook the world he decided to form his own band THE FALL...

Their catchphrase was "WE ARE THE FALL" (it still is), their gimmick was wearing tank-tops and duffle-coats. The early Fall line-ups contained many famous Manchester people who later went on to fame and showbiz....

Soon the FALL attracted the attention of STEPSIDEWAYS RECORDS owned by legendary Punk monetarist MILTON COPELAND who was also manager of a little known pop-punk combo with dyed yellow hair called THE POLICE, who had STRING in them.

Markie Smith soon became pop's MISTER NASTY. He did not like many of the top fave-rave "fashionable" groups of his day. Many a journalist's bottom felt the lash of his tongue (metaphorically speaking)................

GREAT POP THINGS → The Fall Story - Part 2 - They Brought ballet to the masses! BY COLIN B. MORTON and CHUCK DEATH

Over the years the FALL released many "INDIE" records on tons of different indie labels. They left ROUGH RECORDS in protest after Steve Morrissey had claimed that Queen Elizabeth the second of England was, in fact, dead.

Whilst on tour in the U.S.A. Mark met and fell in love with Brix, (later known as the "BONNIE LANGFORD OF INDIE" due to her fantastic singing and tap dancing abilities) It wasn't long before she was a fully fledged FALL member...

Mark wrote "THE POPE WEARS RED SOX" a musical comedy spoof about a nice pope who wants to give the vatican treasures to the poor. The critics, who wanted a straightforward musical like "JESUS CHRIST SUPERSTAR", were baffled.

Unperturbed by the criticism, Markie wrote a "pantomime for rock band and people in tights" called " I AM KOMPLETELY BANANAS "about the life of LUDWIG OF BAVARIA......(Further Fall fun in the future) THE END!!!!

GREAT POP THINGS → THE JOHN LENNON Story "HE TRIED TO MAKE WORLD PEACE BY TAKING ALL HIS CLOTHES OFF" Morton & Death

John Winston Boko Lennon was known as the "first BEATLE" because he thought of the idea and wrote the words, though Paul McCartney got known as the "first Beatle" towards the end of the 60's when things got a bit confused due to "FLOWER POWER" & it's attendant drugs..

Lennon was renowned for his "acid" wit (as in "corrosive" or "burning" & not that he took them drugs or anything). He once astonished the celeb authors at a literary gathering given in his honour with his bitingly WICKED "thankyou" speech.....

Lennon met and wooed the fantastic Japanese Conceptual artist Yoyo Boko. Together they formulated a scheme to take off all of their clothes and NOT put them back on again until there was an end to the VIETNAM WAR ....

Lennon's marraige to Yoyo Boko Lennon was not popular amongst the British people who had never forgiven the Japanese for allegedly "cheating" in WORLD WAR TWO. So the band they formed : JOHN, YOKO AND THEIR PLASTIC BAG" was destined to be "SMALLER THAN THE BEATLES". To be Continued...

GREAT POP THINGS → The John Lennon Story : PART 2 "HE DIDN'T BELIEVE IN THE BEATLES BUT HE DIDN'T MIND THE MONEY" BY COLIN B. MORTON AND CHUCK DEATH

After leaving the BEATLES over an argument with PAUL about who was the "first BEATLE," Lennon embarked on several solo projects, including the fantastic song "IMAGINE" which later became a great hit at the 1987 CONservative PARTY when sung by that Errol Flynn out of HOT CHOCOLATE..................

Eventually John retired from the fab world of showbiz in order to become a "house—husband," living an austere hermit-like existence in a vast New York apartment building. In 1980 he was plotting his return to the world of showbiz when tra-gedy struck..................

After his death a vast "John Lennon Industry" sprung up. Mr. Herb J. Goodman, author of such classic biographies as "Jesus Christ—REBEL WITHOUT A CAUSE" and "MOTHER THERESA—HOT BIMBO from HELL?" was one particularly scurrilous example of this typical early 80's "exploitation"..................

But the spirit of Lennon lives on. Just recently a "scrattie" version of Strawberry FIELDS, set to a pulsating "ACID" beat, stormed the charts and YOYO BOKO still hosts regular televised tribute concerts and tours with exhibitions of Lennon's paintings of people's bottoms and the like... THE END

GREAT POP THINGS → JULIAN LENNON'S SCHOOLDAYS By Colin B. Morton & Chuck Death

Julian was his father's son and it was time for him to leave home and go to an English Public school. He felt a moment of trepidation as the Rolls dropped him off.......

What would the "other chaps" think of him?....When some of the teachers heard that Julian's dad was in the Beatles they asked him to write the school song........

Some of Julian's father's more unconventional and radical 1960's views had rubbed off on him, particularly in such subjects as GEOGRAPHY......................

Julian soon encountered FLASHY, the school bully.....he astonished his chums with his successful ploy of taking off all his clothes and offering "Passive resistance"....... THE END

MILK ADVERTISEMENT BY Colin B. Morton + Chuck Death

GREAT POP THINGS → Sir Scruffy Git M.B.E.: THE BOB GELDOFF STORY

BY COLIN B. MORTON and CHUCK DEATH

Bob Geldoff used to be in the BOOMTOWN RATS, who were so punk that they never took their pyjamas off. They were "new wave" (a type of punk music played by real musicians) and thus unpopular with the real punkrock kids.......

Bob's catchphrase was "I'm looking after Number one". This was an affront to impoverished punk rockers who did not believe in the star-system and reckoned pop stars should use their riches to buy everyone pints...

Another great BOOMTOWN RAT hit was "I Don't Like Mondays" which was about a man in America who shot his wife because he didn't want to go to work. This created uproar among British housewives who feared it catching on here!..

Soon Bob wed TRACY YATES, tattooed daughter of a TV evangelist. They spent their honeymoon in the back of a taxi going up and down the main street of London in the rush hour. As a result their son FIFI TRICYCLEBELL was born..........

One day Bob saw some people on T.V. who had nothing to eat. So he abandoned his "looking after Nº 1" credo in favour of "FEED THE WORLD". He and his pal MIDGE URE out of SLIK decided to make a record and use all the money to buy food.............

So Bob, Midge and their pop star pals recorded a song they had especially written. They used the money to feed starving people in Africa, despite the fears of some fuddy-duddies who wrote to newspapers saying no-one would accept food from a scruffy old git like BOB.

The song was a big number one everywhere in the world, and a special gig was put on with every pop star in the world singing it. During this very special LIVE AID gig BOB became tired and emotional and said the "F" word on nearly all the tellies in the world !!.......

Having thus salvaged his "punk credibility" Bob lost it again by failing to gob on Mrs. Thatcher when she knighted him with the M.B.E. He wrote his autobiography "AM I IN IT?" and retired from the world of pop to make adverts. THE END

GREAT POP THINGS → THE KATE BUSH STORY: She tried to change the world in a leotard!

BY COLIN B. KATEFAN and CHUCK DEATH

Kate Bush had a wild and unbelievable childhood in a windy old mansion with her eccentric parents and her pet UNI-CORN Twinklebrain. Sadly no boys wanted to snog her because they were intimidated by her strange "song-writing" hobby ....

One of the fantastic songs she wrote was called "Wothering Heights," and although she had never read Emily Lloyd-Bronte's book of the same name she had seen an amusing MONTY PYTHON "sketch about it, hence her "semaphore dancing" in the video!

Her 1st album ("a kick up the backside" NME) went straight to number one due to the amazing record company marketing campaign that featured huge posters of Kate and her "baboushkas "down every "tube "station in the country ......

Despite all her success Kate kept her private life out of the limelight and although many pop stars clamoured to snog her she stayed faithful to that Lion bloke off the telly........ sadly, for serious Kate fans, this is **THE END.**

GREAT POP THINGS → THE GENESIS STORY: "Public School Image" by Morton Major & Death Minor

GENESIS attended St. Chadbourne's Public School, where they saved hard from their meagre allowances to buy guitars, mellotrons and theatrical props. However Rock 'n' Roll is not approved of in such conservative establishments, so they were forced to practice in secret........

However they were inevitably found out and had their instruments confiscated and only given back to them after they had "finished the sixth form. So they worked hard, got good A-level results, bought some Range Rovers and set out on 'the road'".....................

Soon they were out in the hard-living, hard-loving world of "the road", and found out that it took more than being able to play your instruments really well and the old St. Chad's tie to make your mark. Then Gabriel had a spiffing idea!

But young Gabriel's idea turned out to be a huge success. However, all was not well and one day their drummer's mum arrived and took him away. They had to find a new drummer AND FAST! But who would it be? (NEXT: ENTER BALDIE!)

Soon Genesis got their new drummer, Paul Collins by advertising in the back of a-well-known-music paper. At first it was feared that Collins would not "fit in" as he hadn't been to St. Chadbourne's Public School......................

However, once they saw Phil's fantastic drumming they soon changed their minds. Gabriel was rather impressed by the fact that he'd played the Arthur Dodger in "Camelot", and frequently asked him for tips on how best to pretend to be a flower.............

Soon, however, Peter Gabriel left GENESIS and started a solo career. So the rest of GENESIS got Phil Collins to use his cheeky chappie "good bloke" gift for impressionism and imitate Gabriel's singing while they looked for a session drummer.......

So Genesis carried on their career with Bill Collins on singing. Pretty soon he embarked on a solo career without leaving Genesis, and all the other members of Genesis did so as well. Meanwhile, Peter Gabriel worked for many charitable causes with Brooce and String.

GREAT POP THINGS → BONGO FURY: the Story of U2 by Colin B. Morton and Chuck Death

Bongo is the son of Sonny Bongo and the famous wooden actress "chair". He named his group **U2** as a clever pun on his parents 60's hit "I love You too Babe".....

When he grew up, Bongo was destined to become one of the biggest megastars ever, along with his fellow **U2** members: The Hedge, Adam Claypole and Ray Perkins.

Their big hit LP was THE YUCCA PLANT produced by Brian Eno who used to be in Roxy music but was chucked out 'cos he couldn't play synthesiser. He did the L.P. using OBSCURE STRATEGY CARDS where you pull one out of a hat and it tells you what to do.........

The U2 became very famous in America when they did a gig on top of PIZZA HUT in San Francisco when all the cars stopped to find out what was going on, Bongo coined his catchphrase, "ROCK'N'ROLL Stops TraFFic"

GREAT POP THINGS → expresso Bongo! U2 Part 2 by Colin B. Morton & Chuck Death

By 1987 **U2** were so famous that the world wasn't big enough to hold all the people who wanted to see them.... So they decided to make a **rockumentary film** called "HUM & DRUM"(after the various noises their instruments gave off when played.)

The plot of the film concerned a hugely famous Irish group going to America and inventing all forms of American music simultaneously. Bongo plays a pop singer called Bonéo who harasses ageing rock stars by phoning them up a lot.

By making their music really boring **U2** united all the peoples of the world, who at last found something they could all understand. As Bongo says "If everyone holds hands and is nice to one another, things will be alright." **etc...etc...etc**

After making several controversial comments about the standard of the acting in SIR BOB GELDORF's Milko advertisements, Bongo was rumoured to be on an **I.B.A.** hit list. He is said to have retired from music to make LP's

DISOBEDIENCE OR JIM JIM MORRISON MORRISON by A.A. Morton x E.H. Death

"Jim Jim Morrison Morrison"
Nanny warned one day
"Do not go close to the edge
When you go out to play"

So Jim Jim Morrison Morrison
Who hated grown-ups' laws
Pulled on his leather trousers
And went off to form THE DOORS

Jim Jim Morrison Morrison
Called the Lizard King
Shocked and amazed his audience
By whipping out his thing.....

Jim Jim Morrison Morrison
Smoked some LSD
Snogged with loads of girlies
And got drunk as drunk can be

Jim Jim Morrison Morrison
Got so big and fat
Had no health-food diet
or anything like that...

Jim Jim Morrison Morrison
Fled to far-off shores
Far away from Nanny
and his Pop-group called the Doors

Jim Jim Morrison Morrison
In the bathtub drowned
(though the doctor who examined him
cannot now be found)

(whisper this:) J.J. M.M.
Is he alive or dead?
So do not go close to the edge
Remember what nanny said

GREAT POP THINGS → Twins of Evil! The BROS story by Colin B. Morton & Chuck Death

Matthew Weston Goose and Damien Lucas Goose were born on the Badhamster housing estate in London... on 6/6/1966. they were looked after by their Aunt LILITH and her faithful pack of savage Rottweilers.

Bros were "unfinished" when they were born! They had no eyebrows or eyelashes or any hair whatsoever and were so ugly that they were **never kissed** like normal kids. They began to crave love and attention.

Despite their intense hideousness the twins became interested in pop music and particularly the craft of songwriting. By the age of 7 they had composed their first rock opera which was performed at their school.

When they reached puberty they found themselves experiencing urges common to most adolescents... they wanted to form a pop group! They recruited some other bloke to play bass and formed an early 80's indie-punk band called PIG BROS.

GREAT POP THINGS → BROS II SATAN'S SLAVES! by Colin B. Morton and Chuck Death

Brilliant but demonically inspired pop songwriters Matt and Damien Goose have teamed up with bassist Andrew Ridgeley to exploit their sublime compositions. Realising the importance of presentation they shun their scruffy past.

Soon they were snapped up by the Epic record label, but abandoned by their massive indie following who felt betrayed because they had "sold out." Confused by this sudden loss of disciples they formed a new plan.

They renamed themselves **BROS** and concentrated on building an army of "wild child" underage girls called "Brossieres" who would buy their records and aid them on the road to world domination....

Their songs became vicious and scathing..."when will I be famous?" was a subversive satire on the cult of personality while "I owe you nothing" taunted the indie-poppers who had deserted them....(more next week)

GREAT POP THINGS → BROS. III THE FINAL CONFLICT By Colin B. Morton and Chuck Death

The brothers Goose are riding an un-stoppable roller-coaster of success and profit. Their nubile army of 13-year-old girls are becoming more confident, more dangerous and more politically powerful..........

For a Christmas single **BROS** record "Unholy Night" and film a video in which they visit the Dark Lord Satan in his diabolic lair. But their game is up, their "luck" is running out.....

Their incredible creativity and hunger for fame turns inwards on them-selves....Bassist Andrew Ridgeley becomes depressed, because he keeps making zillions off all the girlies who keep trying to get a snog off him.

Yea! the power of good is a mighty and formidable thing, and as a recent poll has demonstrated, 1988's summer of love obliterated the memory of **BROS** for ever. THE END †thank God.

GREAT POP THINGS → ACID HOUSE

IT TRIED TO CHANGE THE WORLD WITH IT'S SMILEY BADGES, SHORT-WAVE RADIO NOISES BUT NOT DRUGS!!! By Colin B. Morton & Chuck Death.

In the late 80's a new phenomenon was thrown up.... ACID HOUSE, it consisted of the kids dancing for hours on end to drum machines and noises off the short-wave radio.

The "scratties" as they are known amongst themselves wear "ACID TROUSERS" with 1 straight leg and 1 flaired leg, showing that they have 1 foot in the straight 80's and the other in the psychedelic 60's (except for DRUGS)

Acid housers deny taking drugs, but the "Belpers" (non-acid housers) think they do for some reason. Thus the "smiley" symbol has become as feared as the swastika..... travel agents have had to burn all their brochures.

HOW MANY SCRATTIES DOES IT TAKE TO CHANGE A LIGHT BULB?... ALL OF THEM!! one to change the bulb and the rest to Dance to it! THE END.

GREAT POP THINGS → ACID HOUSE! Why "SQUARES" DISAPPROVE:

Winston Churchill speaks to the nation.......! By Colin B. Morton and Chuck Death

"Look here, um, guys and gals....if JERRY should mount an air-raid this summer you chaps will all just be sitting Ducks stuck out in a field with all those bright flashing lights and whatnot....

And as for garishly-coloured 'ACID-TROUSERS' you hip groovers are wearing, they are just no bally good as Camouflage! Fritz would just mow the lot of you down in a hail of ACK-ACK-ACK-ACK!!

And those blinking WALKMAN devices... you'd be so busy listening to that so-called music you wouldn't hear the bally AIR-RAID SIREN, and the next thing you know your leg is gorn and a dawg is running orf with it over the bombsite! And what about those videos a war could start and you wouldn't see the news...

Thankyou! This has been a party political broadcast on behalf of the conservative party.... THE only Party Worth HAVING!"

NOT TO BE CONTINUED.

GREAT POP THINGS → Madchester: FLARES are BACK! by COLIN B. MORTON and CHUCK DEATH.

huh! how uncool can one GET!

In 1976, the punk rock revolution was started. In the words of pop philosopher Tony Parsons; "Punk changed everything - it got rid of flared trousers!" Now they are back and what we are asking today is WHY?..............

Music MONITOR
FALL JUMP ON MADCHESTER BANDWAGON

THE FALL 'Replicants' ('Phonymer)
With this new album the Fall have jumped blatantly on the madchester bandwagon. By blatantly coming from Madchester, sporting unfashionable haircuts and clothes like their mums bought them etc.

Yes, those very people, who a few short months ago would have laughed at the very notion, are now donning "BELL BOTTOMS," or "LOON PANTS," together with haircuts similar to that sported by ROWAN ATKINSON in BlackADDER ONE.

People Still wearing flares: 1985 Fashion Special
Terry Wogan / A WINO / Chuck Berry / An open University lecturer
HA HA HA Don't these people look silly... not like Spandau Ballet!
BOBBY HELMET OF THE FARCE

At one point in the '80's flares became so unfashionable that even Heavy Metal bands and their audiences stopped wearing them, so why have they returned? Was there a vast surplus in a clothing manufacturers somewhere OR WHAT!!!!?

IT'S the Fashion OF the 90's
...YOU READ IT HERE FIRST POP KIDS!!

What's next? Will the legendary "acid-trouser"(one flared and one straight leg) become fashionable, as predicted in this column? Sources close to THE STONE ROSES reveal the band to be disenchanted with flares so maybe this is the only alternative!

HOW MANY HAPPY MONDAYS DOES IT TAKE TO CHANGE A LIGHTBULB...

UNSCREW UNSCREW UNSCR-SCR SCR-EW
NEW BULBS FRESH FROM THE FACTORY

OK HOLD THIS FOR A MINUTE
FAC 1 BULB

RIGHT NOW PASS ME UP THE NEW BULB

BEZ? SHAKE SHAKE

GREAT POP THINGS → The Dave Bowie Story part 84: THE GLASS SPIDER from MARS tour!

BY COLIN B. MORTON and CHUCK DEATH

In 1988 flushed with the success of his myriad "acting" projects DAVE BOWIE decided it was time to return to his first love – LIVE GIGGING. He decided on a Glam Rock revival 'Glass Spider' tour and built a huge spider made of glass.

First Dave would tell a story about his spider, then he would sing for a bit and do some dancing! At one point he got a girlie out of the audience who seemed all shy at first but later turned out to be an actress Dave had planted there. She did a dance as well!

In a song called "Heroes" Dave said he wanted to sing like Dolphins could sing. This was all a bit odd because Dolphins just make a sort of K-K-K-K! K-K-K-K! noise and jump through hoops. Still Dave is the Chameleon of ROCK.......

After he stopped singing, people clapped for a bit then went home. Dave went home too taking his glass spider with him.....On the way he thought up a brilliant idea to get his glass spider past the man on the bridge ....(TO BE CONTINUED AD NAUSEAM)

GREAT POP THINGS→ The Fantastic DAVE BOWIE Lookalike Contest! BY COLIN B. MORTON and CHUCK DEATH

ZER TIN DREAM!

MIT YOUR LONG BLOND HERR 'N' YER EYES OF BLUE

THE GLASS ELEPHANT!

I DON'T KNOW WHY I LOOK LIKE THIS, MY MOTHER WAS BEAUTIFUL!

OH DEAR I SEEM TO 'AVE GORN OFF COURSE DESPITE MY FAB AVIATONAL ABILITIES

BEETLE JUICE

LYDIA

GROUND CONTROL TO MAJOR GAZ!

ALPHA CENTAURI

THIN WHITE NEWT!

ZIGGY NPARF AND THE WHALERS FROM MARS

COLOURS CHANGING AT RANDOM

Entrant NUMBER ONE : MR. Alf Shikelgruber, a painter and decorator from Paraguay with his version of Dave's mid- 70's "flirting with Nazis" period....

Entrant number two: MR. John Merrick re inacts Dave's hit acting role as "THE ELEPHANT Boy" which was such a big success on BROADWAY.....

Entrant number three: Major Thomas Jerome 'Gaz' Numan Captures Dave's ever popular "Distant Alienated being" Period with this impersonation...

FIRST PRIZE goes to MR D. Jones OF BRIXTON with his excellent "charlatan of Rock".... He wins a Tin machine LP while the runners up win several TIN Machine LP's each ...THE END.

THE DAVE BOWIE STORY Part 127 in which Dave Pretends HE IS FROM SPACE, oddly enough

...and the papers want to know whose skirts you wear !!......

CAN YOU TELL WHAT IT IS YET?

??

BIG ART BOOK

BLIP   BLIP

OUT-UH SPACE-UH weeee cedle weee! REAL NICE-UH PLACE-UH weeeeooooee

COR!!

MISTER THOMAS JEROME NEWMAN, YOU ARE ARRESTED FOR BEING FROM SPACE...

NO I'M NOT I'M AN ENGLISH ROCK STAR CALLED DAVE BOWIE!

OK SING US ONE OF YOUR SONGS THEN BUDDY.....

HA HA HA HE HE HE I'M A LAUGHING GNOME ∝

SARGE I THINK WE GOT US A SPACE ALIEN AN'?

In 1969 Dave started a conceptual bandwagon by pretending he was from outer Space. His Song "SPACE, Oddly" featured "Brain" Eno on stylophone and Rolf Harris on didgeridoo, and was a tribute to the Arthur C. Newman film of the Same name ....

The pretending to be from outer Space bandwagon was jumped on by the likes of cold emotionless Gareth Numan and "the clangers" who were like big mice who nobody knew what they were on about, (A KIND OF WOMBLES FOR FALL FANS).

Sarah Brightman's sexploitative dance troupe HOT GUSSET had their first hit with "I FELL IN LOVE WITH A STARSHIP-TROOPER" and strangely enough Sarah went on to marry the real life space alien pop composer Sir Android-Loid webfoot who owned most of Earth.

Eventually all his pretending to be from outer Space got Dave into trouble when he was arrested in the USA for being an illegal alien. This was documented in his legendary documentary movie "THE MAN WHO FAILED TO ACT"   THE END (?)

Frank Zappa was born in 1940, of normal people like you or I, but, from the start, it was clear that he was an unusual child with a penchant for the musically unorthodox...............

Frank was brought up in Glendale, California, where he attended Antelope Junior High. He, and his classmate Captain Beefheart were not exactly typical all-American boys...............

Despite his tall gypsy good-looks, Frank could not get dates with the teenage schoolgirl contemporaries that were his own age. Instead they all went out with guys who were more regular..........

Frank and the Captain soon realised they did not share the interests of their contemporaries. They were not, in fact, like "the other chaps".....

After he left school, Frank got out of going into the army by making rude noises into a tape recorder. It was deemed that a person capable of such an action was "un-American", and not fit for active service.....

Having failed to get in the army by making rude noises, Frank formed the Mothers Of Invention. Eschewing the effete look of fellow bands of the "flower-power" era, they somewhat resembled a bike gang who had raided a thrift shop...............

Around this time, Frank invented the "FREAK-OUT". He attempted to copyright it by naming the first MOTHERS album after it. He was not, unfortunately able to collect royalties every time someone "freaked-out".....

Parents everywhere were outraged by Frank's group. Unfortunately they could play their instruments really well which accidentally led to PROGRESSIVE ROCK and the TWILIGHT OF COOL which was 1974. ....

NEXT on EMP-TV it's Denzil Zappa and "my mama's going to eat your Guitar!"

LUMPY UNCLE RAT MEAT TAKE TWO... LET'S DO IT GUYS

BRASSIERE!!

ahem

Due to the fact that he was not like other people Frank felt compelled to give his children silly names. Now Denzil Zappa is a rock star in his own right and Moon Utility Muffin Belt is a Video Jock............

In later years, Frank formed many new groups with proper musicians called "Ike" and "Vinny" who played proper session-musician versions of what the earlier demented free-jazz classical avant-garde doo-wop biker group had played...

On a trip to London in the early '70s, Frank and them MOTHERS, which now included FLO and Eddie out of the TURTLES, outraged polite society when they played the ROYAL ALBERT HALL in the presence of Mrs. Betty Windsor, Queen of England........

Eventually a member of the audience, outraged that such foul-mouthed goings on were happening in front of her maj., leapt onto the stage and struck Frank a resounding blow on the temple, sending him tumbling into the auditorium...(To BE CONTINUED)

THE MOTHERS†
AT BILLY GRAHAM'S FILLMORE EAST

PHLO DIAGRAM.......

DIRTY SEX → SONGS ABOUT DIRTY SEX

$ ↑↑↑↑

TV EVANGELIST CONDEMNING SONGS ABOUT DIRTY SEX

TV EVANGELIST SECRET BANK ACCOUNT

INDEED MR ZAPPA TRIED TO BARGAIN WITH THE DEVIL BY OFFERING HIS MORTAL SOUL IN EXCHANGE FOR A SIX PACK OF BEER BUT EVEN BEELZEBUB, THE HOT...

...HORNY DEVIL WOULD NOT ACCEPT A SOUL SO TAINTED

DEAR RADIO MANAGER PERSON,
I'm all in favor of free speech and I oppose any form of censorship like you get in communist countries like, er, Nicaragua (is that still commie honey? But I don't agree with Frank Zappa and I think he should be banned so that people less intelligent than me can't be corrupted by him unless they go into a record shop and listen in one of those booth things do they still got those honey?

I find Frank: ☐ sexist ☐ racist ☐ childish ☐ offensive ☐ not as good as he used to be when he had them original mothers (tick whichever apply)
SO PLEASE BAN HIM. signed................(mrs.)
Wife of veryhigh up well-connected govt. person.... (who knows lots of people who ADVERTISE WITH YOU!!!)
P.S. I don't like that Captain Beefheart either. Except "Blue jeans & moonbeams."
*"Unconditionally."

In the early 80's the phenomenon of T.V. evangelism was thrown up in the U.S.A. Though some of the T.V. Evangelists were interested in GOD and stuff, there were others who just wanted people to send them money so they could afford to go out and do weird kinds of dirty sex......

Frank had nothing against dirty sex, or indeed sex of any kind, but he didn't see why people wished to censor his records, which contained elements of said SEX, in order to publicise their strange T.V. evangelist activities.................

Some T.V. evangelists got wind of this, and this caused them to try and smear Frank with all sorts of things, including how one of his early 78 albums "titties and beer" included references to how Frank had tried to sell his soul to the devil, but even the devil didn't want it, Frank being such a weirdo....

Eventually, Frank attracted the wrath of the Washington wives, who were like the stepford wives, only they weren't robots. They organised a campaign to ban Frank forever....(not to be continued)

GREAT POP THINGS → Political Pop for Girlies → THE SCRITTI POLITTI Story
BY COLIN B. MORTON and CHUCK DEATH.

As a youth in Gwent City (ie Newport) South Wales Green Gartside was "different from the other chaps"

He baffled his teachers by being far more intelligent than them... which was rare even in this particular school...

After his expulsion Green attended Art school in Leeds where he sat around reading his philosophy books.........

Then one day the ACHARNY in the UK tour played the college canteen and Green knew it was time to form SCRITTI POLITTI.....

GREAT POP THINGS → Political Pop for Girlies → THE SCRITTI POLITTI Story

BY COLIN B. MORTON and CHUCK DEATH

PART TWO — actuate the clockwise motion of your record player, thou art Part and parcel of the super-

GREEN
TOM →
NIALL →

SCRITTI
ART

GET SOME SODDIN' ART DONE OR YER OUT!

market of disco discourse "process"

In the cultural melting pot of WILD WEST YORKSHIRE it is 1977 and GREEN Gartside has just formed the cleverest Punk band of all!

Why are you called SCRITTI POLITTI?

"what's in a name That which we call a rose by any other name would smell as sweet"
* shakespeare 1594-95

gulp!

INDIE CHART
1 SCRITTI POLITTI skank block bol...
2
3

So the SCRITS headed for LONDON, where they made the very first "indie-pop" record "Skank Block BOLOGNESE"!.....it was #1!......

JUDAS!

when the government falls, I wish I could tell, la la de dah, sweetest girl in all the world.

Although packs of "SCRITTI-CLONES" such as the Police and RED CRAYOLA were appearing to exploit "clever-Punk" Green wanted...........
...something else.......

How could you give up your indie cred to become such a boring, complacent POPstar??

"a foolish consistency is the hobgoblin of little minds"
RALPH WALDO EMERSON

So he invented "POLITICAL POP FOR GIRLIES", went to America and sat on the beach reading loads of philosophy books...........THE END

GREAT POP THINGS → THE SCRITTI VANILLI Story   By Colin B. Morton × Chuck Death.

...PLATITUDINOUS ONOMATOPOETIC MAGNILOQUENT LEUCOPHLEGMATIC STEGANOGRAPHIC SIGNIFICATION...

EMP-TV AWARDS

he's not really saying them big words y'know..................
HE'S MIMING!

GREAT POP THINGS → MADONNA: Just WHAT is she up to NOW? EXCLUSIVE By Colin B. Morton & Chuck Death

That was IAN DURY doing "HIT ME WITH YOUR RHYTHM STICK"...let's go straight on to your next choice, shall we MADONNA

OK, it's SPANK ME MISTER SHANKLY by Morrissey...

MADONNA APPEARING ON DESERT ISLAND DISCS.

WELL THERE WAS SEAN PENN AND THEN MIKE WATT OUTTA fireHOSE AND SEAN PENN AND...WARREN BEATTY AND SEAN PENN...

MADONNA ANNOUNCES HER DATES TO THE PRESS.

CENSORED!!

MADONNA S RECENTLY MADE A FILM C ED "DICK TRACY" WITH WAR BEATTY, IN WHICH SHE IS "B THLESS" OPPOSITE MR BEA S "DICK"..........

DA! I LIKED DA FOIST CAPTION BETTER

SO DID I

MADONNA HAS RECENTLY MADE A FILM CALLED "DICK TRACY" IN WHICH SHE PLAYS THE FEMALE LEAD "BREATHLESS McGINTY" OPPOSITE WARREN BEATTY WHO PLAYS THE TITLE ROLE. (OK?)

GREAT POP THINGS → MADONNA "SHE TRIED TO CHANGE ORGANIZED RELIGION WITH HER UNDERWEAR OUTSIDE HER CLOTHES" PART ONE BY COLIN B. MORTON AND CHUCK DEATH

I'M, LIKE, COMING TO TERMS WITH RELIGION IN MY OWN WAY

HOW DO YOU SOLVE A PROBLEM LIKE MADONNA?

Madonna Silliccone was born in Brooklyn, a suburb of America's capital, NEW YORK CITY. when she was very young she was sent to live in a nun's coven, however, her wild and rebellious nature made life very difficult.........

DAD I WANNA PIZZA!!!

WELL GO OUT AND GET IT THEN....

CATHOLIC GAZETTE

WHAT A GREAT IDEA

Having become fed up of this austere nun-like existence she went back to live with her dad. she evolved the philosophy that, from hereon in, if she wanted anything she would just go out and get it.........

EXCUSE ME MISS, I'D LIKE TO LOOK AT A BOOK ON THE TOP SHELF PLEASE

OK BOYZ

In her youth she embarked on a string of low-paid jobs to supplement her showbiz ambitions. People who knew her in them far off days reckon that fame hasn't changed madonna one little bit.........

KNICKER GRABBER 3

BIG T SEX

HONEST TO GOD MUN IT'S A LOAD OF ****

Around this time she made the first of quite a few controversial movies.."A Certain Sacrifice," which is so controversial that even the people in the video shop warn you not to borrow it.........
(NEXT: MORE FILM FUN WITH MADONNA)

MADONNA PART 2: "She tried to change the world with these huge black men carrying her about everywhere"

In his epic work of pop scholarship "how do you solve a problem like Madonna" top rock pundit Greil Marcus has compared Ms. Silliccone to Allen Ginsberg, the famed and influential beatnik poet..........

On her neat "Blonde Ambition" tour she told her audiences to all put contraceptives on. It is unknown if this was a genuine Anti-AIDS propaganda campaign or an attempt to annoy the POPE..........

Madonna is famous for having a load of rare private paintings all over her house. One of her favourites is "Madonna spanking the Infant Jesus" by surrealist Paul Eluard... No one who can't understand that painting can be her friend... so there!.....

Madonna's big break came with the movie "desperately seeking Susan" co-starring Rosanna Baquette and that George Harrison from the Beatles..... (NEXT: more and more film fun with Madonna and pals ....)

GREAT POP THINGS → MADONNA: "WHAT'S SHE REALLY LIKE? yawn...." Part 3 BY COLIN B. MORTON AND CHUCK DEATH

In the fantastically successful motion picture "WHO'S THAT GIRL" Madonna played the part of a girl who nobody knew who she was, which was terribly ironic as by that time everybody in the world knew who she was.........

Recently a well-known soft-drinks company gave Madonna $5 Zillion to do an advertisement. Typically she toyed with religious iconography and the resulting video was deemed too "sensitive" to advertise fizzy pop...............

In one of her many rare frank interviews she described her perfect man: a sensitive artist who likes writing letters and painting and has no string of broken relationships in his past, oddly her affairs with Warren Beatty & Sean Penn did not really work out.................

But what is she really like? Will we ever glimpse the private part of Madonna which is kept hidden behind locked doors by burly minders?... Well we tried but the burly minders wouldn't let us so we just had to make a load of stuff up and watch her neat movie "TRUTH OR BED." THE END

GREAT POP THINGS → NIGHTMARE ON ELMS STREET: The SPANDAU BALLET STORY.... BY Colin B. Morton and CHUCK DEATH...

Spandau Ballet was formed in the EAST END of London by the notorious KEMP twins. They held the fashion world in a grip of terror in the 80's, with their accomplices Bobby "THE HELMET" "Elms and Tony "the Kilt" Hadley..................

Style-gurus Kemp and Kemp formed the Spands as a revolutionary ploy to out-wit Mrs. Thatcher. Their theory was; if they could get poor people to look like rich people she would get all confused and not know if she was coming or, hopefully, going..

This failed, however, as the SPANDS like so many others before and since, overestimated Mrs.T's capacity for Knowing when she's not wanted. However, "STYLE WARS" broke out as the new Romanticals fought "posed battles" on each others turf.............

Soon MEDIA-Frenzy was ablaze with the tabloid gutter press exploiting the war-ring TEEN Factions to the kilt. Of course the Spands got the blame as the press is run by capitalists who care not a jot for ART ....

SPANDAU-BULLETS!: "Just when you thought it was safe to go back into the WARDROBE!!"

Despite the incredible "furore" thrown up by the so-called "STYLE WARS" Niel and Nigel Kemp, Tony "the Kilt" Hadley etc..continued to pioneer their TOM-JONES-LIVE-IN-LAS-VEGAS furrow of innovative rock.The HITS JUST KEPT ON COMING !!! And then they stopped................

The KEMPs married fantastic model gir-lies who also had hits. Was there no end to their reign of terror? YES THERE WAS! In 1989 they embarked on an acting career, starring alongside PRINCE ANDREW in ED-WARD LLOYD-WEBFOOTS latest wholly original musical, "EAST END STORY".........

This musical, set in the early 80's, told a Romeo and Juliet type story of forbidden love amongst the new Romanticals. The Kemps were reduced to a mere parody of themselves, no match for a new ruthless generation of twins who cared nothing for the old values of loyalty..........

Had the notorious KEMP twins posed a threat to our way of life or had they just posed? Despite everything there are still some old Romanticals who keep a little place in their hearts for Niel and Nigel.....THE KEMPS!
THE END

GREAT COMEDY THINGS → Andy "NICE" Davis A.K.A. "THE NICE MAN" By Colin B. Morton and Chuck Death

Panel 1: Personally I got nuthin' against gays.... some of these religious types say AIDS was sent to punish homosexuals.... SO HOW COME LESBIANS ARE A LOW-RISK GROUP THEN? Bang goes that theory!....

Whoo, tell it like it IS NICE MAN!!!

Panel 2: Immigration.... this country of ours was founded upon it; there oughtta be a sign at the airport saying.... IF YOU CAN'T SPEAK THE LANGUAGE PHRASEBOOKS ARE AVAILABLE FREE OF CHARGE!!

Panel 3: YOU LOOK VERY PRETTY TONIGHT... YOU KNOW WHAT I'D LIKE TO DO WITH YOU? I'D LIKE TO GO FOR LONG ROMANTIC HOLDING-HANDS & PICKIN' FLOWERS TYPE WALKS WITH YOU but I'm too shy and retiring to ask so my love will have to remain secret and unrequited

Blush!

Panel 4: Gee... I RILLY LIKE YOUR SWEATER!!!

Why thanks!

HE'S NOT MUCH LIKE LENNY BRUCE IS HE?

NO

Caption 1: At the end of the 80's a new comedic phenomenon was thrown up, the so-called "comedy of niceness". Andy "Nice" Davis, one of its chief proponents, is not afraid to tackle controversial subjects in his act.................

Caption 2: Some old-school comedians criticise "Nice" for alleged lack of comedic skills. "He doesn't actually tell jokes," they quibble, "He just says pleasant things about minority groups".... where's the fun in that, eh?".....................

Caption 3: But is the "Niceman" actually that nice or is it all an act? We asked his mother, Mrs Annie "makes good coffee" Davis of Greensboro: "yes he always tidies his room and is constantly running errands for the elderly"........

Caption 4: His tactic of picking on members of the audience and complimenting them on their dress-sense, plus the fact that he comments on controversial issues has led to comparisons with Lenny Bruce................ THE END.

GREAT POP THINGS → Pere Ubu Spot the DIFFERENCE PUZZLE CAN YOU SPOT 3 DIFFERENCES? BY COLIN B. FISH and CHOCOLATE DEATH

1979

THREE cheers FOR MY BIG FEET A BIG HAND FOR these THINGS ON THE END OF MY LEGS!

ZZT TTT BRRP ZZZ

← STRANGE WEIRD LOUD DISTURBING SYNTH NOISES

CRITIC SAY → THIS GROUP IS SO WAY OUT!!

1989

OH WHY DID YOU GO AWAY I LOVE YOU!

STRANGE WEIRD TASTEFULLY SUBDUED SYNTH NOISES

CRITIC SAY → THIS GROUP IS A BIT like R.E.M or them Talkin' Heads

GREAT POP THINGS → Rock Stars in Disguise by Colin B. Morton and Chuck Death

Dave Bowie became so famous that he had to grow a moustache to disguise himself when he went out shopping. The strain of growing a new one every week became too much, Dave stopped shopping, lost weight and became the "thin White Duke Ellington"...........

Jon Bon Jovi, lead singer with the Van Jovi group often wears outrageous disguises to fool his legions of fans, but he is now such a big star and household name that his disguises seldom work and the "kids" spot him and "hassle" his private persona...................

Steven Morrissey of the top Mancunian "Rave" outfit THE SMITHS went as far as getting a job on a building site to escape the hordes of "MOZZETTES" who dog his every step. Impressed by the stoic dignity of the labouring classes Moz wrote "HODLIFTERS OF THE WORLD UNITE"...

Some older Rock stars use disguises to revitalise their ailing careers... for example the TRAVELLING WILBURYS... Who are they? Who would you have in your Wilbury's? SEND YOUR SELECTIONS TO CHUCK AND COLIN RIGHT NOW!.........
(only one dead person per selection please!!)

FANTASTIC NOTTING WILL—BERRIES COMPETITION RESULTS Judges: Morton & Death

TRAVELLING MISERIES!!

TRAVELLING non-ENTITIES

TRAVELLING MYSTERIES

TRAVELLING WANNABEES

Tracy Riley of Levenzoom, Manchester chose this impressive WILBURYS line up: L-R Nico, Laughin' Len Cohen, Morrissey, Nico Cave, Anita Tiktokwoman and wins herself the latest U2 Album..........

Julian Hayman from Gwent wins 2 new U2 LPs for this fantastic selection: L-R Chaz Smash, Paul Rutherford, Andy Ridgeley, the bloke who watches TV in the Pet Shop Boys and Velvet underwear cartoonist Andy Warhol.................

3 or 4 spanking new U2 Discs wing their way to Gill Smith from London for her effort: L-R, A Resident, Womble guitarist Tobermorey, A soup Dragon, the late ELVIS Presley and that car that KLF drove on Top of the Pops with the TIME LORDS........

Mrs. Norman Tebbit of Brixton wins a fab half dozen U2 LPs for this tribute to the girls who would be MADONNA: L-R Debbie Gibson, Marilyn monroe, Kim Wilde, Mand E. Smith and Brix E. Smith, what a great bunch of Wilbury's eh kids?......

GREAT POP THINGS → Punk Artifact #1

I WAS THERE

IF every snotty old punk who claimed to have seen the fab SEX PISTOLS at the 100 Club in 1976 had actually been at the gig, then the 100 Club would have to have been the size of the ALBERT HALL......
Now at last it's your chance to prove that you were there with this EASY TO USE cut out and keep **OFFICIAL** and very **GENUINE** piece of PUNK ROCK memorabilia .... Boost your NEW WAVE CREDIBILITY ......
.... Flash this **AND SNEER!**

CUT HERE ↗

THE HUNDRED CLUB PRESENTS

FEB 30th 1976   21/22 Portobello Rd, BRIXTON

GREBBIE   THEM   Sid's Blood →

SeX PiSTOLS

A&M Recording Artistes +

BONGO + THE SELF ABUSERS (EIRE)

NO HIPPIES! CLASH CITY ROLLERS (Toytown) TICKET Nº 21

EARWAX ← **TWO SHILLINGS and seven d.** GOB

ADMIT ONE - 8·00 Prompt - DRESS 'PUNK'

CUT HERE ↗

GREAT POP THINGS → THE GREATEST STORY EVER TOLD: THE SEX PISTOLS

PART ONE " THEY DIDN' CARE 'COS THEY DIDN' CARE!" BY COLIN B. MORTON and CHUCK DEATH

In the late 70's kids on the streets never had nuffink. The ROCK STARS who had promised to lead a revolution and destroy capitalism with their festivals, etc., were now just a bunch of bloated capitalists themselves..................

The kids on these streets didn't trust no-one. The hippies had now become the "ESTABLISHMENT" with hippie MPs, hippie Archbishops and even a hippie in the royal family! Things were bad for these kids on the streets.

Meanwhile in America's capital, Malcolm McDowell was managing them NEW YORK DOLLS and trying all sorts of dangerous gimmicks e.g. acting a bit like "them ROLLING stones, pouting etc. But the world wasn't ready for them.........

Returning to London McDowell became a travelling rep for a boutique. Whilst on a trip to the provincial blackwoods of Gwent, Wales, he discovered some PUNK ROCK going on there.................

GREAT POP THINGS → The SEX PISTOL Story Part 2 : "I don't want bloody nuffink me" BY COLIN B. MORTON and CHUCK DEATH

On his return to London Malcolm opened his "sex boutique" in the East End's colorful King's Road. It became a "hang-out" for the "kids". He was continually on the lookout for new recruits for his exciting PUNK-ROCK project.................

McDowell discovered some "street urchins" Steve Cook, Paul Jones, Glenn Tatlock and the mysterious and elusive "Wally". They had formed a band with gear that Steve (a "tea-leaf") had "half-inched" off that Dave Bowie.............

DISREPUTABLE GENTLEMAN: "Ah tif a boy and a fine boy indeed what if your name pray?" URCHIN: "I am named John Rotter, fir, and I am fhopping for my poor old mum who haf nothing" GENTLEMAN: "Rotter, what a fplendid name, tell me can you fing?" URCHIN: "No I cannot fir" GENT: "Fplendid, fuperb... would you like to join my fex Piftolf?" URCHIN: "um...
One day Malcolm found Johnny Rotter...

Johnny was taken to the sex boutique and introduced to the other sex Pistols who were practising spitting and playing loud instrumentals badly. Suddenly an enormous shadow blotted out the sun......

(NEXT WEEK: Syd Vicious)

GREAT POP THINGS → The SEX PISTOLS Story Part 3: "Vicious by name, vicious by nature..."

By Colin B. Morton and Chuck Death

The enormous shadow which blotted out the sun belonged to Syd Vicious, notorious denizen of the nether regions. Johnny's new-found chums began to tremble as this monstrous apparition filled the doorway........

It was said that the Kray Twins had confessed their crimes and gone to prison rather than face up to the challenge to their criminal Empire that was Sydney Jerome Vicious. But he loved his mum, Mrs Violent Vicious..........

This was not to be young John's last encounter with the notorious Vicious but meantime he was sent to electrocution lessons to learn how to sing badly enough to match the Sex Pistols music.............

The Sex Pistols "paid their dues" with lots of support gigs upsetting the audiences of respected "old wave" artists such as Sticky George, The Heads of the Valleys, Peris Falsis, Timmy and the House-boys etc.........

GREAT POP THINGS → The SEX PISTOLS Story Part 4: "they shocked the WORLD with their SWEARING on TELLY"

By Colin B. & Chuck D.

The Pistols soon became the bête noir, (or "black sheep") of showbiz. They attracted the attention of EMI records but got chucked off when they threw up all over their contract, thereby invalidating it somewhat.............

Punks were soon following the Pistols example by rebelling against society all over the place with bad manners, eating soup with the wrong fork etc.... Unlike other Royals Princess Anne was a hero to the punks............

Glenn Tatlock one day accidentally turned up for rehearsal and while waiting for the others not to turn up got bored and learned to play his bass a bit. He was immediately replaced by Sydney Vicious..........

They also got thrown off A&M records for swearing on "Blue" Peter Gumby's TV programme which was just as well as Ritchie Wakeman had pointed out that the Pistols couldn't play their instruments really well..................

GREAT POP THINGS → The SEX PISTOLS Story Part 5: The Sound of the Subways
BY COLIN B. MORTON AND CHUCK DEATH.

Next they signed to Virgin a label owned by hippies. It's previous big hit had been Tubular Balls the peace, love anthem from "THE EXORCIST" movie. But Virgin refused to 'play the game' and didn't chuck the Pistols off the label or anything......

The Pistols attracted hordes of imitators and soon the whole "punk movement" was born. Among others, there was the subway SECT who said we are all prostitutes singing songs in prison, Chelsea who wanted the right to work and SHAM 69........

Also, from the north, there was the BUZZ-COCKS (later Buzzcocks PLC), Brix and the Fall, Gang of 4, Victor Vomit who were in stark contrast to today's manchester groups such as them whacky happy mondays.............

"Rock'n'Roll God Save The Queen" the English national anthem was released AND BANNED by the B.B.C. 'cos the electrical guitar backing was said to be "sexually arousing" and made people have "disrespectful" thoughts about her majesty........ (TO BE CONTINUED)

GREAT POP THINGS → THE SEXY PISTOLS Story Part 6: ENNUI IN THE UK!
BY COLIN B. MORTON AND CHUCK DEATH

List of REAlly Important Things Done By PUNK:
1. Caused girlies to have fantastic shavedy bits on the sides of their heads
2. Got rid of HIPPIES for a bit!
3. Got rid of FLARED trousers for a bit!!!
4. made studenting MOST unfashionable. BY A. JOURNO.

Various people accused the Pistols of callous commercial "cashing in" on the Jubilee, with it's noble patriotic garden parties, baloons & funny hats. It is a little known fact that McDowell and the Queen "stage managed" the entire event to attract more publicity.............

Soon the Pistols were banned from everywhere in Great Britain, Europe and the world so they had to resort to various subterfuges like touring secretly as the Barron Knights (a well-known comedy group who did amusing Sex Pistols skits)..........

The Sex Pistols album "Bollocks To Everything" went to the top of the charts, beating off opposition. Charged with "rudeness" they won their case when a vicar said the title reflected an anti-materialistic way of life..........

The Sex Pistols became the cause celebre of pop music journalists who envied their youthful zits, vigour etc.....and wrote things like "punky rock is very very important....it got rid of flared trousers etc."

GREAT POP THINGS → SEXY PISTOLS PART 7: THE BOY WHO ASKED FOR MORE!
BY COLIN B. MORTON & CHUCK DEATH

Then disaster struck: Syd Vicious fell in love with a girl called Nancy. This was causing trouble for the group as it was making Syd all soppy and girlie. He wanted to start playing the acoustical guitar instead of chopping people's heads off......

Having been banned everywhere in Britain the PISTOLS went to America so Syd could meet his prospective in-laws. They did not approve of him, his outrageous punk rock life-style or his cute English accent............

Johnny Rotter, however, was growing discontented with the punk philosophy of nihilism and swearing. He decided to approach McDowell with a view to broadening the band's scope and getting more royalties on spitting...........

Soon Johnny Rotter quit the PISTOLS and formed the PUBLIC IMAGE Ltd with Jah Wobbliehand and Keef Levi's (EX-CLASH). They sung weird atonal songs of mind-numbing despair.....

GREAT POP THINGS → THE PISTOLS STORY PART 8: The Great Rotten Punk Rock Swindle
BY COLIN B. MORTON & CHUCK DEATH

TEN PUNK COMMANDMENTS
① Lots of Spitting
② If you see something you don't recognise... SMASH IT!!
③ NO FLARES!!!!!!!
④ HATE ALL ROYAL FAMILY EXCEPT PRINCESS ANNE
⑤ Hair nice and short like teacher says....

With singer Rotter out of the band, Malcolm made a movie with Julian Tenpole Tudor. Syd was mostly too soppy girlie and in love to be any good, so it was up to Paul Jones and Stevie Cook to do the acting in it.................

So the sexy Pistols ground to a halt, a sad parody of itself, lost and unloved, wasted and washed up. Syd got took away to heaven by a white Rolls Royce at the end of Malcolm's movie.

Johnny Rotter is still very angry. He said so in "The Observer". He is however still on the Virgin Record label with his PILL group, so although he thought he didn't have a future he, ironically, did really...........

In the late 80's the Sexy Pistols were temporarily reformed with that Glenn Tatlock, Steve Cook, Paul Jones and Axolotl Rose...... This did not last a really long time. THE END i.e. NO FUTURE!

GREAT POP THINGS → HIP HOP RAPPING : The MUSIC OF the 80's BY COLIN B. & CHUCK D l.a.m.f.

THIS IS ME, MUHAMMAD ALI, I FLOAT LIKE A BUTTERFLY, STING LIKE A BEE, IF HE TALK JIVE HE FALLS IN FIVE, IF HE TALKS SOME MORE HE FALLS IN FOUR!!

WE THE U.S. ARMY HEREBY ARREST MR. ALI FOR REFUSING TO GO TO VIETNAM and SET FIRE to babies in their prams

The very first person to do "rap" poetry was the great boxer-poet Muhammad Ali. He would recite poems about how he was going to "whup" his opponents, about how pretty he was, how great a poet he was etc. He also wore boxer shorts and shoes with funny tassels.........

This is we, RUN DMC, we're good at rapping poetry, we are the best MC you'll ever see, and other things that rhyme with E !!!

This had a direct influence on "rap". The main lyrical concern of "rap" singing being how pretty the "rap" singers are, and how good they are at "rapping". Although they weren't boxers many "rap" singers liked to wear boxer shorts and training shoes with the laces undone........

I AM HERE TO TROUBLE YOU !!!!! I AM OVERLORD W !!!! I DRIVE ROUND IN MY BMW....er, that's it.

THIS IS ME DJ * I AM.. .... oh bugger

Certain letters of the alphabet are more "hip" than others due to their innate rhyming capacity. There exist obscure examples of HIP HOP RAP DJ MC's whose careers were mercilessly cut short by choosing the wrong letter of the alphabet at the outset! ....

WE SEND THE WATER DOWN the TAP — AND WE Take away YOUR CRAP!

This is the PRIVATIZATION RAP !!!!

Soon HIP-HOP RAPPING caught on due to the fact that anyone can do it and because every word in the English language rhymes with another one. It is frequently used on T.V. adverts by the likes of Leslie Crowther and other "celebrities"........ NEXT WEEK OBSCURE & WEIRD MUTANT strands of HIP-HOP!

GREAT POP THINGS → HIP HOP RAPPING : The MUSIC OF the '80's BY COLIN B. & CHUCK Dee

Pass me a screwdriver CHUCK

Why we like MRS THATCH

One technique of the music used to accompany HIP HOP RAPPING is "scratching" using "samplers". These are compilation albums containing all sorts of different music. RAP D.J.'s after the sound of these by "scratching" them, leaving them out of their sleeves, exposing them to sunlight etc.

OH PRINCESS FERGIE, Large of LIMB, with Freckles & red hair, You're marrying Prince ANDY, I hope I shall be there.*

* From Johnny B's Banana B-B-Blush

Among the little-known precursors of HIP HOP rapping was SIR JOHN B. (Betjeman). Far from being a street-wise kid on the street, he was a little balding man what looked like a teddy-bear. He was Poet Laureate to Liz 2, Queen of England and invented "Ruralist RAPPING" using brass bands........

THIS IS ME PROFESSOR ME I WORK FOR THE OPEN UNIVERSITY BUT THERE'S ONE THING I'M WONDRIN' 'BOUT HOW THEM DINO-SAURS DIED OUT .!!

Eventually hip-hop rapping became so widespread that the OPEN UNIVERSITY on B.B.C.2 started lecturing in a hip-hop fashion. One such example is the series "THE DINOSAURS: DID THEY FALL OR WERE OR WERE THEY PUSHED? conspiracy theory!" in the Jurassic Age...

DID A BIG METEOR COME FROM SPACE? PUFF ROCKS 'N' DUST all over the place SO PHOTOSYNTHESIS could NOT take place? DID SMALL MAMMALS eat their eggs? DID they eat so much that their legs COULDN'T carry them ABOUT? I'VE HEARD ALL THE M.C.'s I'VE HEARD THE BEST! AND NONE of them can stand the TEST AND COME UP WITH A THEORY 'BOUT HOW the DINOSAURS DIED OUT !!!!!!

NEXT WEEK: Great pop things examines the career and philosophy of one of the greatest hip-hop rapping groups PUBIC ENEMY in part 3 of this in-depth series "HIP HOP RAPPING" the MUSIC OF the EIGHTIES !?..we certainly hope so!

GREAT POP THINGS → GREAT HIP HOP THING: PUBIC ENEMY

"THEY TRIED TO MAKE BLACK AND WHITE PEOPLE LIVE TOGETHER IN PEACE AND HARMONY BY SEPARATING THEM!"

Public Enemy named themselves after a terrific pun, so that if they had a number one hit record there would be headlines in the papers saying "PUBLIC ENEMY NUMBER ONE." However they never had a number only, one 9, 37, 12 and other such numbers of the alphabet.............

For a gimmick, PUBIC ENEMY started carrying POP-GUNS on stage as a metaphor for urban violence. Influenced by the teachings of pacifist philosopher LOUIS FAKKARAKKARAN, they tried to separate all the black and white people in their audience...............

However, all the black and white people did not particularly want to be separated as there was enough trouble what with SMOKING and NON-SMOKING parts of the theatres. Eventually PUBIC ENEMY abandoned this policy and became very popular despite all their daftness....

Professor GRIEF the mild-mannered DJ and ace diplomat had to leave the band in 1989 when his brain exploded during a bus journey through North London. Band leader CHUCK D. retired to draw childish cartoons for the RECORD MIRROR... THE END.

GREAT POP THINGS → D.I.Y. GENERIC RAPSPLOITATION MOVIE by Colin B. Morton and Chuck Death....

NOW LISSEN UP...I want you to stop selling these druuugs to the kids plus you're gonna gimme all yo' ill-gotten gains so I can put on a hippety-hop rapping concert to show the kids a good example!

"Things are tough in the ghetto. There are only three ways to get rich...hippety Hop rapping music... dealing drugs and ....boxing..... BOOM BOOM chick BOOM BOOM CHICK BOOM BOOM chick WAH WAH WAH WAH BOOM BOOM etc...

YES BUT I HAVE THE POWER OF HIPPETY-HOP RAPPING... plus I was a junior golden gloves champion before I renounced violence.....Malcolm X ....Martin Luther King....etc......

BOOM BOOM CHICK BOOM BOOM CHICK!! "...AND SO THEY PUT ON A BIG HIPPETY HOP RAPPING GIG AND ALL THE GHETTO LIVED HAPPILY EVER AFTER. THE END" coming shortly: Vanilla Ice cleans up a posh suburban ghetto by organizing a neigbourhood watch scheme.................

GREAT POP THINGS → DURAN DURAN: They tried to change the world by dressing UP!......

PART ONE BY COLIN B. MORTON and CHUCK DEATH

Duran Duran were a new Young Romantical group in the early 1980's. They would scoff at the drab "industrial" clothes that were fashionable then. Eschewing this, they chose to dress as fops and dandies of the regency period...

Having so much more style than everyone else DURAN DURAN decided to form a group and name it after the man who invented SEXY BAGPIPES in the erotic underground cult 60's SCI-FI movie BARBARELLA....

Their debut hit "THIS IS PLANET EARTH" really told it like it was. Other groups were thrown up like SPANDAU BALLET and Steve Strange's BRADY BUNCH. Even established stars like DAVE BOWIE and LIBERACE got in on the act by dressing up as clowns and running along beaches.

But then tragedy struck! Whilst on a ski-ing holiday in Switzerland the Duran Duran group accidentally skiied into a glacier and were never seen again.....(for a bit).........
MORE NEW ROMANTICAL FUN NEXT WEEK

GREAT POP THINGS → DURAN DURAN: They tried to change the World with their yachts. Part 2

By COLIN B. MORTON and CHUCK DEATH

Last week as you will remember, top New Young Romanticals DURAN DURAN fell off a cliff, into a glacier and were frozen in a block of ice while ski-ing in the Swiss Alps. Now read on....

Our heroes are thawed out in next to no time and soon discover that it is 1988! they have been in a state of suspended animation for nearly six years: THEIR SKI-SUITS ARE HOPELESSLY OUT OF FASHION !!!

On their return to Great Britain Duran Duran had no way of earning an honest living so they were forced to eke out a meagre pittance on the NEW YOUNG RO-MANTICALS GLAM ROCK revival circuit.

Then they had the brilliant idea of reversing their name. Now called Duran Duran, instead of Duran Duran, they put out a new record "BIG THING" and hoped no one would remember them from the first time. Nobody did, it was a hit, and Duran Duran were BACK! THE END

GREAT POP THINGS → THE Pet Shop Boys: one sings, the other watches telly. BY COLIN B. MORTON and CHUCK DEATH

Niel and Chris were two boys who worked in a pet shop. They were in love with pop music and spent their time making up tunes. This frequently got them in trouble with the man who owned the pet shop!

Pretty soon they got the sack for making up tunes all the time and not selling any animals to people. The man who owned the shop just DIDN'T UNDERSTAND THEM as is often the case with SQUARES and "the kids"

But once they were out of the shop, a man approached them, He said he had been listening to their tunes in the shop and pronounced them jolly good. He asked them to make a record and be on TOP of THE POPS

They had so much money they didn't know what to do with it all. So they decided to buy the pet shop, as it was where they felt most at home making up tunes. But that didn't please the man in charge! THE END

GREAT POP THINGS → The TRANSVISION VAMP story: SHE TRIED NOT TO USE HER SEX OBJECTS AS SEX OBJECTS..... By Colin B. Morton & Chuck Death.

Transvision Vamp consists of a woman called Wendy James and 3 or 4 blokes. (we are not sure how many as they don't get in the photos very often. Mostly there are just pictures of Wendy refusing to use her objects)

The word TRANSVISION does not appear in the dictionary, but if it did it would come between "TRANSVESTITE" and "TRANSYLVANIA". VAMP means "an improvised chordal accompaniment" or "a woman who utterly refuses to be a sex-object (honest!)".....

It is a little known fact about TRANSVISION VAMP that they have also made records, one of which was quite famous last year or maybe the year before. It had a video of Wendy refusing to be used as a sex-object.

All Wendy's efforts to be a non-sexist object proved to be in vain due to the "gutterpress" who cared not a jot for her artistic integrity while giving lavish coverage to the musical creativity of such "male" bands as Bros. It's all wrong you know!

GREAT POP THINGS → The LED ZEPPELIN Story PART ONE: "THEY'D PLAY THE BLUES... ONLY PROPERLY !!!!" BY COLIN B. MORTON AND CHUCK DEATH

In the late '60s LED ZEPPELIN exploded onto the scene like a blazing blimp. Their influence is still felt today, what with bands like the CULT and the MISH with their hair like girlies and dry ice (CO_2) see pic..........

It all started when Jim Page, guitarist with teenybop group The Yardbirds noticed that American blues chappies were not playing "THE DEVIL'S MUSIC" properly He decided to form a group and jolly well show them how it should be done; so prog rock was BORN!

He recruited a group of like-minded musicians in order to play the blues, only properly. They were; BOBBY "Percy Planet" Plant, ex-of the HOBBIT boys, French philosopher Jean-Paul Sartre on bass, and Bonzo the Dog on drums...

Because their name obviously created a little confusion, they decided to change it. At the suggestion of MOONY LOONY, who was famous in the 60's for throwing T.V.'s out of windows, they became "LED ZEPPELIN"

"DID THEY SELL THEIR SOULS TO THE HORNY ONE? (except the BASS PLAYER...)"

The story so far; Led Zeppelin have worked up a fantastic repertoire of original Pagey/Plantey compositions, (MANY OF WHICH HAD PREVIOUSLY BEEN COVERED BY U.S. BLUESMEN SUCH AS HOWLIN' WOLF AND WILLIE DIXON-WHO, HOWEVER, DID NOT PLAY THEM "PROPERLY") But the magic ingredient of success still eluded them......

At the suggestion of their manager, Peter Granite, Jimmy Page hot-footed it to the library and got a load of occult books out. Using these, they allegedly sold their souls to BEELZEBUBBLE, except Jean-Paul Sartre the Bass player, who was an existentialist and a bit suspicious...

However, despite rumours being rife in the pop world that they had sold their souls to the devil, the elusive hit single eluded them. However their first 3 LPs "one" "two" and "three" respectively topped the charts, selling a staggering 222 million copies each...............

Despite having been able to think up brill titles for their first 3 albums, they were stuck for what to call the fourth one. So they put a load of prunes on the front. This contained their classic Thatcher putdown "Stairway to Heaven" (TO BE CONTINUED)

GREAT POP THINGS → THE LED ZEPPELIN story Part 3: "Valhalla OR BUSt!" BY COLIN B. MORTON AND CHUCK DEATH

In 1974 Zep recorded a Gospel L.P. called "HAMMER OF GOD" about how they renounced BEELZEBUBBLE after exchanging mickey mouse watches with ELVIS PARSLEY at his Graceland mansion in Memphis......

After years and years of Rock'n' Roll mayhem Led Zeppelin finally went their separate ways. Bonzo the DOG finally went to the big kennel in the sky, years of liquid lunches having finally taken their toll on his system...............

Jean-Paul Sartre went back to being a famous session-musician who nobody had heard off, whilst Jim Page composed soundtracks for occult film maker KEN ANGRY's diabolical silent movies...........

Percival Planet went back to Wolverhampton and lived in an Iron Age village, before launching his solo career. Zep still occcasionally reform for special events like LIVE AID or someone's birthday............THE END

GREAT POP THINGS → The WOODSTOCK CUCKOOS:

ARE THE 90's THE 60's UPSIDE DOWN? HIPPIES ARE BACK !!!! what went wrong? a G.P.T. social anthropology readers guide

By COLIN B. MORTON and CHUCK DEATH

PRELUDE: SAN QUENTIN CRISP CORRECTIONAL FACILITY U.S.A. CIRCA 1989

I'M WALKING BACKWARDS TO MANCHESTER ENGLAND ACROSS THE IRISH SEA

WITCHY RAYS

Well all basic respiratory & motor functions check out OK. How long's he been like this?....

OH, A FEW DAYS NOW

Those of us teenagers who remember the 60's, remember interminable sundays with nothing but religion on TV and our mums doing the ironing. Those of us who do not, thru the miracle of PROCESSED NOSTALGIA preceive the 60's as a golden age of jolly nudie people dancing in jelly etc..........

IT'S SAFE TO COME OUT NOW THE PUNKS HAVE GONE!

CULTURAL REFUSE DE

You may have noticed recently........ HIPPIES ARE BACK! But where did they come from? Did Doctor Who bring them from the 60's in his Tardis? Did someone find them in a skip? Have they finally noticed that punk is over?.......................

DEATH MIGHT be your LIBRARY CARD

In the 60's the youth of America was set on fire with flower-power frenzy. Loads of self-styled "Hippies" "dropped" "out" of their society and went to San Francisco at the behest of such bands as the Grateful Dead, but now HIPPIES ARE BACK!...................

HIPPIES.. ARE THEY DEMONSTRATING A NEW LIFESTYLE OR ARE THEY JUST TRAMPS WHO TAKE DRUGS? ARE THEY THE BLUEPRINT FOR AN ALTERNATIVE SOCIETY OR ARE THEY JUST PLAYING SILLY BUGGERS IN A FIELD? ...JEREMY GET THE CAMERA ON THAT NAKED "BIRD"!

OK Bunny

Why have they "dropped back in"? The answer to this question, which affects all of us teenagers, is far more bizarre than you can imagine. Today's HIPPIES are not the ones you see on 60's documentaries holding "BE-INS" (see above) at Altamount, but are in fact .....THEIR CHILDREN !!!!!!!!!!!!!!

GREAT POP THINGS → HIPPIES ARE BACK!

Panel titles / speech: "OH DEAR GET MANSON HERE AT ONCE WOULD YOU CLINTON DEAREST?" — "YES MR HOOVER" — "QUENTIN CRISP I HATE EVERY INCH OF YOU, BUT HATE IS LOVE SO THAT MEANS I LOVE YOU TOO! DOGS ARE CATS, DAY IS NIGHT, COLOUR T.V. IS IN BLACK AND WHITE HELTER SKELTER GOO GOO GOO JOOB!" — WITCHY RAYS — strum strum — 666 — HOW TO SPOT A HIPPY KID — name: "RIVER" "THORIN" "GALADRIEL" "ELROND" — EYES: like in midwich Cuckoos or Gaz Numan videos... "PLASTIC HENGE" made of Lego — LORD OF THEM RINGS HID BEHIND A DIRTY BOOK... MUSKY — HELTER SKELTER — "THIS IS CRAP! LISTEN.. THIS IS CRAP!!!" — JONI mit-CHULL — "OOOH I WISH I WASN'T A RICH POP STAR... SO I COULD PLAY FOR FREE IN THE STREETS"

It is a little-known fact that "flower-power" was a diabolical experiment jointly performed on all of us teenagers by, among others, the record industry, the CIA, Elrond Cupboard, Harry Krishnas and Charles Manson. Then the "flower children"'s programming went wrong and they started killing movie stars......

In order to find a scapegoat, the CIA "fitted up" Manson, saying he was the sole instigator of this mayhem. He has languished in SAN QUENTIN CRISP PRISON, America, for nigh on two and a bit decades, under constant observation........

Meanwhile, all the other hippies in the world, who had been let off by the judges in exchange for "grassing-up" Manson, got "straight" jobs as school teachers, social workers and such, wore suits and raised their hippie kids

By utilizing a sort of Mansonesque "reverse-conditioning-disorientation-training" the hippies raised their children to pass undetected amongst us normal people... (NEXT WEEK in "HIPPIES ARE BACK!" the conspiracy unfolds + Beach Boys tour dates).....

GREAT POP THINGS → HIPPIES ARE BACK!! Part three THE WOODSTOCK CUCKOOS

Panel speech: WITCHY RAYS — "...er I'd like some cigarettes please... oh, and some cigarette papers, cannabis?" — "charlie is my darling" — BUS STOP — "Hey man you don't eat toast 'cos you wanna eat toast, you eat toast 'cos society conditions you to eat toast..." — WOODSTOCK THEME PARK → — "hey man the bus is gone" — "FAR OUT" — "are the 90's the 60's.... ...upside down?" — NME — Sham96

Dear Chuck & Colin, I HEREBY APOLOGISE FOR NOT GETTING RID OF HIPPIES LIKE I SAID I WOULD, yours sincerely, Lester Bangs. Sidney Vicious. Johnny Rotten-Lydon. Julie Burchill. Frank Zappa. Frankie Vaughan. — N.B. FRANK SINATRA DECLINED TO SIGN THIS, A SPOKESMAN SAID, "IF FRANK WANTED TO GET RID OF HIPPIES THEY'D BE GONE."

Suddenly the sons and daughters of the original hippies, who, up to now, had appeared to be normal like you or me, began to behave rather oddly.... strange powers were at work...............

Suddenly everywhere you looked there was this new generation of saddly (sorry) hippies spewing forth their laid-back philosophy and questioning conventional values...............

The "bank generation," those of us who came of age between the first lot of hippies and the 2nd generation, now find ourselves sandwiched between two separate lots of hippies...............

Acoustical guitars are still classed as musical instruments,.... Charlie is due out soon, Simon & Garfunkel infest the charts.... We hereby demand an apology from all those pop stars who promised us they'd get rid of hippies forever!

GREAT POP THINGS → The VANILLA ICE Story: "HE WAS A MEAN BLACK DUDE FROM THE GHETTO even though he was white......" BY COLIN B. MORTON and CHUCK DEATH

Vanilla Ice was brung up in the ghetto of Miami Beach. Life was tough for the young Ice, even though it was quite a nice ghetto with a fabulous coastline and excellent bathing facilities...............

The son of legendary blues singer Blind Lemon Ice, Vanilla spent most of his childhood lying around in this ghetto eating ice-cream whilst his father composed blues songs about having no job to go to...

Ice soon earned the contempt of the other kids at school because, despite the fact he was white, he was black. Held up to ridicule for his street argot, patois and ragged clothes, his mum mrs. Cherry Ice had him "bussed" to Harlem......

Here things were a little better as Vanilla found kids of his own colour except that he was white. He had difficulty mastering the art of hippety-hop rapping, however. Until, legend has it, one fateful day............

VANILLA ICE "the meanest toughest kid on the BLOCK except for BART SIMPSON..."

So the story goes, Ice mysteriously vanished from school one home time, and when he came back the next day he could hippety hop rap like no one's business. soon he had written a fantastic rap called "Ice, Ice baby"...

Ice took his rapping song to a record company where they thought it was so good that they got Dave Bowie and Queen to do the backing. This is commonly thought amongst blues-rock scholars to be not unconnected with the "awful price to pay" (see #1)

So now Ice is the biggest rapper on the hippety-hop (The music of the 80's) scene and has loads of fantastic girl-ies chasing him. There are, amazingly, still some who doubt that he is a tough black dude from the ghetto like he says...............

To combat the doubts and allegations of the unfaithful Ice recently went as far as revealing his various duelling scars during an interview on the Jimmy Carson show...........

THE END

~~CLASSICAL~~ GREAT POP THINGS → THE NIGEL KENNEDY STORY: "HE TRIED TO CHANGE THE WORLD WITH HIS CLASSICAL MUSIC, FOOTBALL & SLANG"

By Colin B. Morton and Chuck Death

Nigel was raised on the Badhamster housing estate in London's rough-and-tumble East end. As a teenager, his chief loves were playing the violin and supporting his beloved ACCRINGTON STANLEY football team. He thusly spake a colourful argot, a kind of "Cockney classical slang."...

A child prodigy, Nige won "Opportunity Knocks", a TV programme that nurtured fresh new talent, beating off such stiff competition as a 'housewife' playing the spoons, a bloke who painted himself silver and wiggled his bottom-muscles and Bonnie "screaming Lord" Longford....

He used his grant from "Opportunity Knocks" to go and study violin in New York's famous "School for the performing Arts" home of the notorious "KIDS from Fame" from which stems his fashionable dress sense and media-friendly extrovert behaviour...............

Whilst in New York, he "hung-out" in Greenwich Village, observing various jazz/bohemian/folk/beatnik/performance art happenings like Jimi Hendrix did before him. From this evolved the flamboyant style which has made "NAZZA" whatever he is today...

"HE OUTRAGED THE CLASSICAL ESTABLISHMENT WITH HIS TRENDY "WITH IT" GEAR AND PUNK ATTITUDE!"

On his return to London, Nige shocked the "proms" audience with his flamboyant punk violinist gear and his antics such as setting fire to rare "STRADIVARIUS" violins and smashing them against the conductor's rostrum.............

His concept-LP "Nige plays the Four Seasons" topped the indie charts after JOHN PEEL accidentally played the whole of side 3 "THE FALL" on Radio 1. Thus he had succeeded where Fred Mercury, ELO, ELP and ELQ failed, in bringing the works of old dead guys to all us teenagers........

Throughout his teen years "Nazza" had spent all his time fiddling in his room & had nothing to do with "chicks." However, he soon made up for lost time when he captured a "monster animalette" BRIXIE SMITH (who was married to MARKIE SMITH of the Fall) in his Accrington Villa boxer shorts...

The Kazza-Brixie relationship was to cause quite a stir in the popular press. One sunday tabloid alleged that Nige would forego snogging Brixie before a "classical gig" in order to, ahem, "channel all his energies" into his violin !!!!!!!!

THE END.

GREET POP THINGS→IGGY and the STOOGIES By Colin B. Morton and Chuck Death

In the 1960's when everyone was protesting against Vietnam with their flowers, The Stoogies burst upon the scene like a zit, showering peanut-butter over the parts of their complacent hippy audience.

Iggy would also show audiences his horrible bottom, an activity not in the repertoire of Donovan or the MAMAS and/or the PAPAS. They soon got a record out called "NO FUN"...."It certainly isn't," said the critics!....

The 2nd Stoogies LP was called "FUN HOUSE" in a vain attempt to get the critics to say "It certainly IS!"...this didn't work, however, except in the case of Gonzo VICK SIN-EX addict LESTER BONKS.........

Eventually, frustrated by the lack of success shown by their records, the STOOGIES all split up and got proper jobs, except for Iggy who got put in a loony bin because he couldn't stop showing people his bum.

GREAT POP THINGS→IGGY POP: "IGGY is helped by Dave!" By Colin B. Morton & Chuck D.

Along with many others, such as ANDY WARHOLE and WILLIAM BURroughs, Dave Bowie was an admirer of IGGY's enormous talent. So it was really no surprise when Dave plucked Iggy from the bottom & made him a star!

So Iggy's third record, "Raw Power by Iggy and the new stoogies" was made in the U.K. where Iggy went "on the road" and made personal appearances. This formed the basis of "Punk Rock" with it's nihilism and bad grammar.

However, The "Raw Power" LP did not sell very well so Iggy decided to split up his Stoogies and make a series of DAVE BOWIE influenced records with Dave Bowie. This did not go down very well with true Iggy fans........

However, "Live" on stage the Iggy is still the firebrand he always was. Just recently in NEW ZEALAND he did a tour sponsored by a "well-known soft drink", where he showed his horrid bottom to just about everyone.

GREAT POP THINGS → WORKING OUT WITH IGGY— By Colin B. Morton and Chuck Death 💀 💀

HOWDEE FOLKS IGGY HERE!

WELL I LIKE TO KEEP IN SHAPE Y'KNOW.... AND MY NEW WORK-OUT MANUAL WILL ANSWER ALL YOUR QUESTIONS ON HOW I DO IT

Yes Using my unique method, YOU TOO CAN HAVE A BODY LIKE MINE!

COMING SOON..........
THE IGGY POP-UP BOOK
next in this series— MICK HUCKNALL's beauty TIPS and "vitamins I have loved" with KEITH Richard.

GREAT POP THINGS → The BRUCE SPRINGSTEEN Story: "OH NO THEY'VE Shut the Steelworks!"

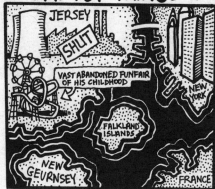

Bruce Springsteen was BORN IN THE USA in Haight Ashbury Park, Jersey. This is not so much a park as we know it, more a sort of vast derelict funfair. It's not known which ride his "mom" was on at the time of his birth.......

As we know from his songs, Bruce spent his early years running all night thru dark streets at the end of town, to the consternation of his "mom" who worried about him "hyperventilating" like Americans do at these moments.......

Brooce first fell in love with rock'n'roll when as a small child, he saw the legendary Elvis Presley being filmed from the waist down on T.V. He made a puppet called "Little Elvis" and played a baseball bat in front of a mirror............

Sing this in a gravelly voice: "One day Broooce bought a guitar/Sung some songs in a local bar/the audience all shouted 'hurrah'!/they said the boy was gonna go far/along came a man with a big fat cigar/say 'sign my bottom, you'll be a star!'"

HE TRIED TO CHANGE THE WORLD BY GIVING HIS WEALTH AWAY

In the early days, Brooce struggled in different groups of all shapes and sizes such as Dr. Zoom And the Sonic Boom, which turned into the slicker more glamorous sounding BROOCE SPRINGsteen AND HIS E-STREET GANG

His record company thought they had found the new Bobby Dylan, which was good news 'cos everyone had got fed up with the old one. They flew him to London amid great consternation.............

John Landau of Rollin' Stone said his famous quote "I have seen the future of Rock 'n' Roll and it is called Broocce" Loads of Bruce-imitators with snappy street-like names began to appear and Landau became Broocce's manager....

His hit "BORN TO RUN BACK TO THE USA" told about Vietnam veterans disillusionment upon returning to America only to find ⒶThey'd lost ⒷThey were out of work as the steel works had been shut down.................

GREAT POP THINGS → THE BROOOOCE Story PART 3: "Born to RUN AND RUN AND RUN etc...etc

Bruce was known as the hardest-working man in showbiz. His audience was full of nurses and coal miners all going "Isn't he hard working?" and "yes he's got a nice bum as well".....

Bruce is renowned for his philanthropizm, playing masses of benefits for other superstars. In 1984 he got into trouble for giving money to the UK miners' strike........

Some say BROOCE's not the all-round good guy of our mythologies. Some of his loyal employees lost his canoe and exposed him as an avaricious tyrant when he asked for it back as he was very fond of it......

Despite being a "Blue Collared" type of chap who never had nothing at all, Broooce was known as "THE BOSS" which is one down from being "THE KING". This demonstrates the complexity of the U.S. class system.

GREAT POP THINGS → TIN MACHINE : "Be Yourself, whoever that is!" By Colin B. and Chuck D.

In 1989 Dave Bowie returned to his Classic "Laughing Gnome" period. He formed a group, "TINY MACHINE", which had guitar, bass and drums & NO GIMMICKS such as glass spiders or plants in the audience.......

Dave recruited Rip Geiger-Counter on guitar and also the great bass and drum duo Huntoon and Snoopy Sails, who had worked on Lou Reed's "ROCK 'N' ROLL" LP where he did FaB Heavy-metal versions of Velvets songs.

The album featured the name "THIN MACHINE" in big letters on the front and Dave Bowie's name in little letters on the back. People soon realised it was Dave however, due to the low-key series of interviews and the low-key T.V. special ....

Dave grew a beard specially so that no-one would recognise him on the front of the album, which featured his great version of JOHN LENNON'S "I'm a WORKING CLASS HERO." Dave changed the words slightly so that he personally could "relate" to them more !!!

GREAT POP THINGS → On TOUR with the TIN MACHINES! er that's Dave Bowie, actually, readers but keep it quiet eh what ?...........

BY COLIN B MORTON AND CHUCK DEATH

As we have seen in a previous episode, Dave Bowie returned to his classic "LAUGHING GNOME" period in a hush-hush low key operation called TIN MACHINE in which he imitated one of his childhood heroes — JIMMY PURSEY of SHAM 69 and did everything himself "FOR THE KIDS".......

Besides opening doors for himself, he also drove the van himself, sold tickets and programmes himself....he even tried dressing up as a nurse and looking after himself but this proved unfeasible as even DAVE, chameleon of rock, cannot give himself the kiss of Life!

Unfortunately for Dave, he was saddled with a "rider" from his old days as a "SUPERSTAR" prior to becoming the "ordinary chap", he is today. This meant he had to sleep in boring luxury hotels whilst the other chaps lived it up in true Rock'n'ROLL style by sleeping in the VAN!

Dave has some difficulty with his all-star American bandmates whilst on the road as they don't understand his typically BRITISH sense of humour and he likewise doesn't understand their American jokes.......MORE DAVE SOON !!!

GREAT POP THINGS → St. Valentine's day Special by Colin B. Morton × Chuck Death

GREAT POP THINGS → ROCK N' ROLL: The Music of the DEVIL? A G.P.T. info service by COLIN B. MORTON and CHUCK DEATH

Recently a leaflet crawled into our hands which has distressing implications for all us POP KIDS... it infers that ROCK is a mere tool in the hands of the DEVIL! Can this really be ?............

This disturbing leaflet's understandably anonymous authors assure us that the names of many famous pop groups are in fact SECRET CODES for naughty things put there by BEELZEBUBBLE!

Yes, even so-called "CHRISTIAN ROCK" stars are not exempt from this. Does not the new easy-to-read English Bible itself not say "stay away from the discos, Satan is out to get you" (PETER 5-8 ....it says here)?

So remember kids, stay away from "Christian Rock" by the Christians, do not take drugs and NEVER play your records or CD's backwards! (all excerpts from a real leaflet found on a bus, honest!)

THE END

GREAT POP THINGS → The ROLLING STONES 50 years in SHOWBIZ Special! Part ONE
BY COLIN B. MORTON and CHUCK DEATH

The ROLLING Stones were formed in 1939 by Alexis Corner, a BBC news-reader & amateur BLUES singer. At first they were not a great success because his cut-GLASS OXBRIDGE accent was not right for the VOODOO rhythms of the DEVIL'S MUSIC"...............

So they sacked him and got Michael Jagger, a Cockney spiv with a degree from the London School of Economics (which helped him to understand the plight of the poor Black Folks of the U.S.A.) on VOCALS and HARP.....

Soon the youth of Britain was caught on fire and the cry went up: "Would you let your daughter, baby, marry a ROLLING STONE?" "Comedians cracked jokes about them, such as, "Have you seen that MICK JAGGER? Hasn't he got BIG LIPS, HA HA HA!" "..........

Soon moral indignation was rife when it was revealed that the band had been arrested for going to the toilet in a public convenience. (in the 1930's many Victorian people did not go to the toilet even in the privacy of their own homes! (TO BE continued)

GREAT POP THINGS → The ROLLING STONES 50 years in SHOWBIZ Special! Part TWO
BY COLIN B. Morton and chuck DEATH

In the 1960's the ROLLING STONES were said to be "always a half an hour behind the BEATLES" Because of this they "missed the bus" when the psyche-delic flower-power era happened. However they still had parents everywhere Vomiting into their cream of chicken soup!

Keef Richards was runner-up "wild-man of pop" to mick. Influenced by old blues songs like "I gotta have a jelly roll", he ate so many sweets that his entire body rotted away from the teeth downwards and he had to have a new one built ....

Brian Jones was 3rd prize "wild man of pop", with a commendation for raffia-work. He was to die tragically in a bizarre Pooh-Sticks accident in A.A. Milne's swimming pool. He is now an even bigger cult than when he was alive (it is not known if he will be on the 1993 tour...)

Mick Jagger decided to turn his hand to acting and was considered to have talent rivalling even that of Dave Bowie or Sting. In Alex Roeg's "Per-formance" he played a gangster who dis-guises himself as MICK JAGGER and sings some songs .....(TO BE CONTINUED...)

Don't quit BILL !!!

Bay City Rollers fans →

← St Winnifred's Girls School

WOODY

he's up there with Hockney in my book

genesis Porridge

23

Brian

altamont theme usher →

Angels

GREAT POP THINGS →The Rolling STONES 50 Years in SHOWBIZ Special! PART THREE

BY COLIN B. MORTON AND CHUCK DEATH

OOO!

UH, Am I too Loud Fellows? I SAID AM I... oh, never mind, sorry

Plink! Plink!

During the 70's and 80's the Stones did nothing of interest, only made records. After Brian's death they had many guitarists, including MICK 'Dick' Taylor. The "Quiet man of pop", most people didn't even realise he was ever a stone until their back catalogue was re-issued on CD......

...and now at number seven it's NAPALM DEATH with 'JARGONISTIC TERMINOLOGY ALIENATES THE PROLETARIAT'

This isn't real music, there's no tune, NOT LIKE THE ROLLING STONES

AAARGHUH UH UH OOOWFFR OOOWFFR GUH BABB! BBAAB!

TOP OF THE POPS

OH MOTHER YOU JUST DON'T UNDERSTAND

Eventually they replaced him with WOODY of the legendary BAY CITY ROLLERS, the so-called "Tartan terrors" from Scotland. By now the Stones were bastions of the establishment, as the punk rock and new Romantical revolutions threw up ever more outrageous new acts......

THE Sun

COR!

THE PAPER THAT'S STILL BOBBIN'

STONE IN 2-IN A BED SNOG

MANDY BILL →

WE SAY IT'S DISGUSTING THAT AN OLD MAN LIKE BILL WYMAN SHOULD HA-

KER AFTER A YOUNG (see Pic.) MINI-SKIRTED (see Pics page 2 and 3) GIRLIE LEGGY RANDY MICE-SMITH (see centre pages) SAID "NO COMMENT ABOUT HER RELATIONSHIP WITH... (continued over)

ALSO IN TODAY'S SUN those luscious AGE 3 GIRLS! Some cartoons where peoples clothes fall off !!.....

But then at the height of their respectability DISASTER! OUT-Bloody-RAGE! BILL WYMAN one of the notorious "one of the ones at the back" was alledged to have snogged a girlie called MANDY RICE-SMITH. He topped the charts with his solo single "ROMAN POLANSKI'S WAITING".......

FALSE TOOTH ROADIE! GET IN HERE NOW !!!!

MIND MY ! ZIMMER!

LOCK UP YOUR Mothers! THE ROLLING Stones WORLD TOUR 1989

Where am I?

ROLLING STONES

DRESSY ROOM

Rumour has it that the ROLLING STONES will go on tour again so watch out kids, it could be your mum or younger sister who falls victim to the lusts of these profligate PENSIONERS, these wrinklie wastrels, sensualist senior citizens, DODDERING DON JUANS......er....

mick's Healthy New image →

♪ you know your mama ♫ fed you on mung beans sold in the market down in NEW ORLEANS oooo! Brown sugar... better for you that white oooo! ♪ white sugar made keef stay up all night ♪

Keef's solo spot →

Who can take ♪ the sunrise and wrap it in a dream ...the Candy man ♪ can !!! ♫

WOOARGH!! I've hurt me finger...

'ere Keef man you 'aven't 'urt one of the ones yer play guitar wiv 'ave yer man?

yeh I've hurt one of them two

GREAT POP THINGS → The Kids New On The Block Story: PART ONE

BY COLIN B. MAURICE AND CHUCK STARR

One day, Gonzo Funburger and his folks pulled up roots and moved to Columbia, Ohio. Gonzo was very, very nervous about moving to a strange town. Would he make a whole bunch of new "buddies" easily?...........

Unbeknownst to Gonzo, a "whole bunch" of other new kids were about to be moving onto the "block"; Emmett "Animal" Schroeder, Ephrem Xyxycroff AKA "Piggy", Kermit and Robin Dweazil-Unit and Fozzie Van Vliet - They were all KIDS NEW ON the BLOCK!

Yes, Gonzo Funfunburger and the new chums he had "gotten" soon discovered a mutual interest in hip-hop-rapping (THE MUSIC OF THE 80's) and in no time at all they'd set the music biz on fire with "HANG LIMP" and other songs that examine the problems of pre-pubescent teens!...

But there were some who claimed that K.N.O.B. were mere puppets and "tools" in the hands of the music industry. Was this true? Or was it inverted racism from music critics who like their oppressed minorities to be from poor, hard-done-by minority groups? TO BE CONTI-NUDE!

K.N.O.B. SHOOTS UP CHARTS Part 2 "REBELS WITHOUT NO CLOTHES!"

Despite feeling the rough edge of many critics' tongues, "KIDS NEW ON THE BLOCK" were soon top of the charts everywhere in the world. Imagine! Already the top selling band of the decade and it's only January 1990...(see graph)............

As pop music is infested with evil capitalists who care not a jot for art, it was not long before the vultures hovering over the industry, their beaks ever open for the kids' cash began to exploit K.N.O.B. with cheap money-grabbing "gimmicks"................

However K.N.O.B. were still the teen-age rebel bête noirs (Black sheep) of the establishment. By indulging in such wacky pranks as taking off ALL their clothes and leaving them in other artistes' dressing rooms they soon earned the nickname "NUDE KIDS ON THE BLOCK"

CREDITS

ALL WORDS BY K·N·O·B. composed by Maurice S.

ALL MUSIC BY K.N.O.B. composed and played by M. Starr

A MAURICE STARR PRODUCTION BASED ON AN IDEA BY MAURICE STARR

K.N.O.B. WOULD LIKE TO THANK MAURICE STARR FOR HIS VALUABLE GUIDANCE THROUGHOUT THEIR CAREERS......

Mr Morton's hair by Maurice Starr

Mr Death's dietitian Dr. M. Starr

REPENT HARLEQUIN!

GREAT POP THINGS → The ANITA TIKTOKMAN Story: SHE TRIED TO CHANGE THE WORLD WHILE DOING HER 'O' LEVELS!! by COLIN B. MORTON & CHUCK DEATH

Tania Tiktokoman was not interested in midnight feasts in the dorm or crushes on prefects. Instead she listened to Joni Mitchell going on about how crap it was being a rich pop star snogging lots of pop stars.

RIGHT, THAT WAS A SONG ABOUT HOW THE PIGS OFFED SOME OF THE KIDS AT KENT UNIVERSITY, 'COS THEY WOULDN'T GO IN AFTER PLAYTIME.......

and this one's about WOODSTOCK where half a zillion Kids stood in the rain for 3 days without no clothes...

WOW HOW SINCERE.

Tabitha Tiktokperson soon realised it was quite easy to do this herself, so she did a gig in the Tight Fiddler, Neasden & was rocketed to the top by people who wondered how one so young could have so much whinging SELF PITY in her...

VOT IS IT DARLINK

SPURT SPURT

THE ELVIS I KNEW WAS NO TRANSVESTITE !!! HIGH COURT JUDGE TELLS ALL

SUNDAY SPURT ELVIS IS ALIVE AND LIVING IN BASINGSTOKE AS A WOMAN

phone some Girls up for some PSY CHAT

So great was Tanika Tanktopbottom's resemblance to the LATE Elvis Presley (ONLY thinner, with a wig on) that a series of Elvis sightings were reported around her home in Basildon Bond, Hampshire.

TWISTIN' MY SOBRIETY AWAY !!!

PIZZA

Tirana Teknocratic's big hit was "twisting my sobriety" by Chubby Checker. Such was her fame that she took to fining people £50·00 if they got her name wrong. (that's why we've been so careful)

GREAT POP THINGS → The SISTERS OF MERCY STORY: they tried to change the world by pretending to be DEAD!

DUE to strange juxtapositions of slagheaps, tower blocks and factory chimneys, the North of England (specifically Leeds) gets only one hour of daylight at four in the morning when it's dark anyway and everyone is ill or asleep………

This causes a strange, not-dead, not-alive but both condition known as "**GOTH**". The leader of "Goth" is Simon Taylor-Garthwaite AKA Spiggy Eldritch. His sense of the dramatic never allowed his "Goth" image to slip.

Rumours that Eldritch fronted the infamous transvestite Irish traditional showband THE SISTERS of MURPHY are unconfirmed, but big things lay ahead for this mysterious and spooky pint-sized popster!

His ambition had always been to have a group that could play 18 minute long versions of Dave Bowie's ironic Death rock anthem "THE LAUGHING GNOME" so he formed **THE SISTERS OF MERCY** to be continued

"BREAKING UP up up IS HARD TO DO.." → the SISTERS of MERCY "Gothic Rock" story Part 2

Spiggy Eldritch's SISTERS OF MERCY are riding high in the GOTHIC charts with hits like "TEMPLE OF DOOM" & "ELECTRIC OCTOBER" but constant touring and occasional exposure to daylight starts to take it's toll….

Imitators like ROSIE AVALANCHE, FIELDS OF THE HEFFERLUMP & THEN JERICHO have started to outsell the Sisters even though they lack any trace of _real_ GOTH credibility (i.e. humorous cover versions.)

To the horror of their fans the SISTERS split up. Andrew Oldwitch claimed to own the words "SISTERS" and "MERCY" so the others formed a group called "THE OF." Eldritch swiftly released an LP under the name "OF THE."

Now the SISTERS are a duo featuring Spiggy Aldridge and Morticia Morrison (ex-"BAGLADYS" and "PUDDING CLUB") who was engaged to stand silently in the background on all the sisters records and videos.

THE HERB J. GOODMAN STORY: "only the name has been changed to protect the GUILTY!!!"

Australian-born Herb J. Goodman sold his thriving colonic enema parlour in London's Earl's Court to finance the publication of his "ELVIS: VOODOO SEX ZOMBIE" in which he claimed that Elvis had been killed in action during the Vietnam war and revived by his manager Colonel Sanders using chicken's blood..................

Despite the critics constantly claiming that his horse was a butterfly Goodman went on to write "UP AGAINST THE WALL, WHITEY: the Mahatman Gandhi story" in which he claimed that Gandhi had suggested the idea for the second world war on the back of a Christmas card he sent to Adolph Hitler way back in 1938..................

Other little-known works by Goodman include "NICE GUYS FINISH LAST: The Joe Stalin story", "MOTHER THERESA, Hot Bimbo from Hell", and "Jesus Christ: Rebel Without a Cause" which was filmed by RUSS MEYER with Dennis Hopper in the title role, Kitten Natividad as mary magdalene, and Marianne Faithful as the virgin mary..................

His return to the exacting science of post-contemporary biography was "Smiling Assassin: the life of John Lennon" in which he postulated than Lennon was a serial killer who had bumped several people off by hitting them on the heads with shovels... This was denied by his widow Yoko, ex-Beatle Paul McCartney and one of his alleged victims.

THE BILLY BRAGG STORY → "ROCKIN' AND ROLLIN' AROUND THE RED FLAG!"

As a youth Billy "Mr Bignose" Bragg could not get a snog off a girlie, no matter how he tried. Then one day, on a bus, an event took place which was to irrevocably alter the course of his life, (forever)..............

For a long while Billy was in the stores in the army, which is a really difficult job consisting of nothing but calling things "backwards" to confuse the enemy. Then one fateful day the call to action arrived....

At Greenpeace common Billy spent many days and nights guarding the defenceless U.S. cruise missiles from the fierce "WIMMIN" of Greenhalgh common who would adorn the fence with knitting & other witchy symbols of "female power"

Having never snogged a girlie (see: "THE WICCA MAN" starring Edwood Woodwood) Billy soon fell prey to the "weird sisters", "earth energy" and it wasn't long before he started acting all girlie....which ill-befits a member of the armed forces....

BILLY THE BRAGG Part two: HE TRIED TO CHANGE THE WORLD WITH HIS MASSIVE GLASNOSE!"

Having been physically attacked by the cosmic peace and love earth mummy vibrations of the GREEN PEA COMMON women, Melvyn Bragg was caught, marshalled and chucked out of the army for subversive "nice" tendencies.....................

Once in "CIVVY STREET" Billy could not get a proper job anywhere because it said on his army report card that he was a dangerous subversive who supported organizations like CND and the Labour Party...then inspiration struck!

So Billy approached GOGO DISCS with his idea for a rock version of the "red flag", in no time at all he was on T.O.T.P. alongside people like that bloke who used to take his clothes off on the soap powder advert. Bill was also big on chat shows......

Whis his fantastic cover of KARL MARX's "RED FLAG" topped the charts in Russia, Bill paved the way for "GLASNOSTRIL" a new era of peace between nations, in which girlies would rather snog popstars rather than members of the armed forces...THE END.

The POP WILL EAT ITSELF Story: "They tried to change the world with their gentle whimsy!"

"Lerruz in oiv bin plide on John Peel"

STOURBRIDGE ART COLL. ENTS SOC. SOCK HOP

Pop will eat themselves came from Stourbridge where they were much-loved, respected members of the community. A few years ago they made a record which was almost a hit and got played on "John Peel" a few times......

"I can't find any mate!"

Can't find any? what mate.

I can't find any mate in this food!

vegetarian buffet

Soon they were touring and they got on swimmingly well with other groups who admired their conceptual brilliance in ripping off SIEG SIEG SPUTNIK. Also they impressed with their happy-go-lucky wit and quaint old-fashioned attitudes to the fairer sex.......

I've GOT whales of stale, w-w-whales of stale, I am bad and ill, i think late a stalemate pie, then I drank a kippertie

DIFF! BONK! WHIZZ! SOAR!

Eventually they became the first white people to invent hip-hop except for the BEASTIE BOYS. They did a tour with PUBIC ENEMY whom they admired so much that they wrote a song called "Beaver Patrol" as a tribute to them.....

ALAN MOORE KNOWS THE SCORE, He's writing a comic about a superstore AUF WIEDERSEHN PET, CAN U STILL GET IT?

PWEI were not popular on the tour. Was it inverted racism or was it because they are crap? Who can really say. Anyway they soon bounced back with "CAN U STILL GET IT?" a list of things that were vaguely trendy in 1986.
er... THAT'S IT!!!

THE GARETH NUMAN STORY: HIS FRIENDS WERE ELECTRIC!.....PART ONE.

Bleak ashen Gareth was born plain GARRY WEBB. Even as a baby he was emotionless and dispassionate. He did not cry when the doctor smacked his bottom as he was too busy listening to the faint "BLIP-BLIP" of a distant electro-cardiograph.......

As a boy his only friends were a pop-up toaster called Bobby and a microwave oven named Timmy. His favourite pirate radio station was the short wave, and he would only watch the television if it was "ON THE BLINK"........

Gareth first displayed musical ability when, on holiday with his family, he entered a talent-contest with his own radical re-interpretation of that well known summertime standard "oh I do like to be beside the seaside"!

When he grew up Gareth decided to have a group. As he had no chums except Bobby and Timmy he built himself an army of robot Tookalikes in the garden shed. He named them TUBEWAY ARMY after the well known Cockney saying "the tubes are full of computers"

GAZ NUMAN Part Two THE TUBES ARE FULL OF COMPUTERS....

Last week, as you will recall, GAZ E. Newman formed a group consisting entirely of robots. With these he made his first record "My Friends are Electric". Unfortunately nobody bought it except Timmy the microwave and Bob the toaster, so GAZ built himself an army of Robot fans called NUMANOIDS

Pretty soon Gaz was riding high in the charts, and his house was constantly beseiged by NUMANOIDS who chanted their robot adulation. In order to get out of his house unscathed GAZ had to save up & learn to fly an aeroplane!.......

Unfortunately Gazza's first flight was a complete disaster and despite his vast aviational skills he crash landed in India where he was detained by the Indian secret police who thought GAZZA was a SPY!!! (shock, horror).........

Gareth now lives as a recluse, and still likes robots and dislikes human beings, even to the extent that he votes TORY! He has no girlie friends as he is afraid they will snog him or "tell all to the newspapers...THE END

GREAT POP THINGS → The JiVE BUNNY Story: 2 FINGERS UP TO THE CRITICS! BY COLIN B. MORTON and CHUCK DEATH

Humphrey and Bernard Pickles were two lads from PUDSEY in West Yorkshire. Both were keen DJs and they noticed that medleys of old records all joined together went down well at church functions, fêtes and the like and it gave them an idea.....

So the two chums decided to take their idea for records made out of bits of other old records all stuck together to the record companies down in London, but time after time they were shown the door by the designer-moguls of the then fashionable "80's"......

But fate played the straight-man, when they went to RSPCA/Telstar, a visionary company with a visionary A×R Dept. who had been responsible for signing such original talents as the late great ELVIS PARSLEY and the chameleon of rock Mr Dave Bowie............

Soon all the nation was going crazy mad with JIVE BUNNY fever or "MIXERMATOSIS." The little kiddies went mad for the rabbit, (which only they could see) and the old people went "ape" over the old records (which only they could remember) but trouble was a-brewin'.....
(next week: BACKLASH!)

GREAT POP THINGS → JIVE BUNNY and MIXERMATOSIS PART TWO BY COLIN B. MORTON × CHUCK DEATH

YES WE KNOW WE USED THE MIXERMATOSIS JOKE LAST WEEK BUT WE'VE RE-MIXED IT THIS WEEK. IT'S DIFFERENT, IT TAKES A LOT OF EFFORT, PEOPLE THINK IT'S EASY...

As we saw last week, Jive Bunny and their comical Celtic marsh-spirit or "POOKA" were now the toast of Britain with their records made out of all other people's records stuck together. But trouble was brewing from the self-styled "teenagers" in the 18-40 age bracket

Having been pandered to for all these years by STYLE-BIBLES such as THE FARCE and the Neo MISERABLE EXPRESS the so-called "hip-groovers" were now more than a little "miffed" that the little kids and old folk had a "scene" of their very own!

However there were others who did not hesitate to jump on the JIVE BUNNY bandwagon. Ex-Playboy BunnyGirl Deb Harry made a comeback and several imitations such as "JIVE COCKROACH sings the Blues" and "JIVE SLOTH sings the NICK CAVE songbook"...

GREAT POP THINGS → JOHN PEEL DOWN THE AGES part one: SCHOOLBOY IN DISGRACE

BY COLIN B. MORTON and CHUCK DEATH

Just 'Cos I'm a stranger everybody dogs me round!

I say the music emanating from this "Duke Joint" is jolly fine

TAP TAP

1959; John Piers Ravenscraft is exiled to the colonies, having disgraced his well-to-do parents by failing the special "easy O levels" designed for members of the Aristocracy & royalty. He is sent to study cotton picking in the southern states of the U.S.A. ....

DONNY HELP ME, DONNY DONNY

CAN YOU JUST HOLD THIS FOR THE CAMERAS?

EXHIBIT A: LEE HARVEY OSMOND'S SPECIAL SHOOT SOME CORNER GUN WITH PERISCOPE SIGHT

HI I'M MARILYN KENEDDY O'NASISS AND YOU SURE DO HAVE A CUTE ACCENT, GEE etc...

er...

1963; BEATLEMANIA! Keneddy assassinated! Somehow fate makes these twin phenomena thread together to make young 'Ravenscroft' a D.J. megastar! On attending the press conference of alleged assassin Lee Harvey Osmond he is hired as a "Beatle Impersonator" for U.S. Radio.

WHADDAYA GOT TO SAY ABOUT DIS MISTA LENNON?

WZRB CHICAGO

← our hero

ER.... GEAR FAB, YEH Turn left at Greensboro... WILL THAT DO?

DARK BLUE PLANET BEATLES INSULT GOD, MOM APPLE PIE AND THE FLAG!

1966; His career as a Beatle impersonator comes to an abrupt end when John Lennon scandalises America by suggesting U.S. kids would rather listen to pop records than go to church. The Beatles are slung out of the U.S.A. Peel fulfills his contract by becoming a D.J.

HERE'S THE MOTHERS OF INVENTION FROM 'ONLY IN IT FOR THE MUMMY' OOOPS WRONG SPEED, OH NO IT ISN'T, I REALLY SHOULD HAVE GOT THE HANG OF THESE RECORD PLAYERS BY NOW YOU KNOW I WAS GRAMOPHONE MONITOR AT SHREWSBURY....

MY GOATS BEYOND

mantovani JOHN McGLOCK ORCHESTRA

SURREALISTIC TOILET

JEFFERSON AND LAKE PALMER

SAFE AS RECORDS

WZRB CALIFORNIA

DRUGS ARE REALLY BAD FOR YOU GRATEFUL DEAL

1967; The SUMMER OF LOVE. John changes his name to Peel at the insistence of his guru and hosts a psychedelic programme in SAN Francisco. Here he discovers Captain BEEFHEART, who will make TROUT MASK REPLICA, the best record ever, don't you think !? TO BE CONTINUED...

JOHN PEEL Part 2: "He transformed the art of D.J.ing by being interested in POP RECORDS!!

1967; Peel flees the U.S.A. in terror when someone with a clipboard asks him if he can remember where he was when Kennedy was shot. Back in the UK. he lands a job on the pirate ship called RADIO LEIGHTON, doing THE PERFUMED GARDENING SHOW............

Soon all the pirate radio ships sink in the ocean 'cos the D.J.s are too busy playing records to splice them mizzens and that. Peel gets a job on RADIO ONE where his revolutionary policy of playing records instead of just talking about himself, makes him TOP D.J.

1968; Peel tops all D.J. polls, despite the fact that nobody likes the music he plays, 'cos all the other D.J.s just open supermarkets, and tell jokes about their wives leaving them. This is the time of the "PROGRESSIVE ROCK" Boom...........

1974; The progressive-rock boom leads inexorably to the TWILIGHT OF COOL that is 1974. All the groups Peel has championed in the past now make double-albums with orchestras reading joined-up music to prove they got the "O" LEVEL. Peel who has no "O" level is disillusioned...

JOHN PEEL DOWN THE AGES → Part 3: "HE PLAYED MUSIC PEOPLE HAD NEVER SEEN BEFORE"

1976; Having long grown disenchanted with "PROGRESSIVE" music which he didn't understand 'cos he didn't have the O-level, Peel embraces "PUNK". He sends his special MBE. prize back to the Queen and his effigy is burnt onstage at a JEFFERSON LAKE and PALMER gig...

The 1980's: Due to the jealousy of all other Radio One D.J.'s Peel is mercilessly shuffled around throughout this decade so that no one know's when he's on. Sales of RADIO TIMES reach all time high due to loyalty of fans, but he still suffers abuse from "progressives"...

1992; Sales of genuine John Peel memorabilia now common; The sitar he smashed and the Everton F.C. kit he wore on his notorious Top of the Pops appearance with the FACES fetch many zillion quid plus V.A.T. each. Sales of his late sixties prose poetry are still slow.

1997; Having been so long in showbiz, Peel now shows signs of extreme wear and tear and terminal confusion sets in. He keeps getting his career of D.J. muddled up with his T.V. commercial voice-overs. As a result he is given a RADIO ONE Afternoon slot! THE END

GREAT POP THINGS → THE STRING STORY part one THE POLICE STORY "THEY TRIED TO CHANGE THE WORLD BY DRESSING UP AS POLICEMEN" BY Colin B Morton and CHUCK DEATH

SIR! CAN I HAVE A NEW EXERCISE BOOK?

OF COURSE NOT THEY'RE MADE FROM TREES!

The Police emerged during the anarchic post-pubescent "PUNK" era. Stuart COPland having previously been in "FRIJID AIR", Andy Sumner having been in a version of the "SOFT MACHINE" with none of soft machine in it and GORDON "string" summers having been in a dead end job IE. scholeteachering (of which more later).........

I SAY STRING YOU'RE HOLDING YOUR GUITAR THE WRONG F*** ING WAY ROUND

NO I AM THE H*LL NOT DO YOU WANT A FIGHT?

BRILLIANT

OK LADS YOU'VE GO THE F*** ING GIG !!!!

Having formed a group called "THE POLICE" they found to their dismay that they could PLAY THEIR INSTRUMENTS REALLY WELL, which was unfashionable due to PUNK. This was a big problem so they pretended not to able to play their instruments very well in order to get some 'GIG' bookings.............

NEEARG

I HEREBY ARREST YOU FOR IMPERSONATING AN OFFICER OF THE LAW, ANYTHING YOU...

HM Police Notepaper

I LIKE SEX PISTOL

In the seventies there was a quaint custom of naming your group after an occupation or hobby E.G. The Tourists, The Bank Clerks, Sailor, Queen. But they were forced to give up their gimmick of dressing as policemen after an embarrassing incident when they were arrested by plainclothes police dressed as hippies.

TRUST ME!

NEW WAVE COMMANDMENTS
① PLAY Instruments REALLY WELL
② no swearing unless it's in really Long WORDS ie. "masturbators" "coprophiliac oedipus complex person" etc

Drummer Stuart Copland was brother of MILTON Copland who invented "PUNK MONETARISM" IE. taking money off "THE KIDS" and keeping it. He and Stuart were the sons of MILTON COPLAND SENIOR who wasn't in the C.I.A. Stu got his brother to manage the POLICE....
(TO BE CONTINUED)

"THEY TRIED TO CHANGE THE WORLD BY DRESSING UP AS PUNKS A BIT ONLY NOT REALLY...."

THE WILL GRUNDY SHOW!

GO ON, SWEAR, CUSS, BAD-WORD!

NO WE SHAN'T

WE HAVE INVESTED OUR MONEY WISELY IN BUILDING SOCIETIES.

Thus and as we have seen, the "NEW WAVE" movement of which the POLICE were part, was like PUNK except for two very important factors:
① NO AGGRESSIVE BEHAVIOUR OR SWEARING!!!
② INSTRUMENTS ARE TO BE CARED FOR & PLAYED REALLY WELL AT ALL TIMES.........

A GOO GOO GOO A GA GA GA GA GA GA.... there, that's much better than all that nonsense about Haile Selassie and stuff N'est ce pas

Money money money money money money money money money money money

Taking the "NEW WAVE" ethic of removing the interesting bits out of popular music styles in order to improve them, the POLICE invented a kind of REGGAE, only without the "toasting" or "DUB" bits. They replaced these with STRING's fantastic lyrics..........

YOU'D FORGET YOUR OWN HEAD IF IT WASN'T SCREWED ON WOULDN'T YOU BLENKINSOP?.. YOU'RE YOUR OWN WORST ENEMY AREN'T YOU?......

NO, MY worst enemy is Timms minor in 4R

STRING was often accused of being "pretentious" having named all the POLICE albums in French I.E. "Regatto De Bank", " Le synchronitique." He was also accused of having "no sense of humour" because he hated being called "STING." It is a well known fact that teachers are very humorous.

Don't come- Don't come- Don't come too close to me
Don't polish your shoes too much or your underwear will be plain for all to see

Although STRING and the POLICE became very famous and rich they were also "controversial" In the song "Don't Come Too Close To Me" STRING drew on his experiences teaching the facts of life to school children without mentioning sex. After the savage media backlash STRING disappeared up his ORINOCO....

At this time of year, many of you will be embarking on, for want of a better word, "careers" as art students. Here is a step by-step guide to the often baffling world of "art studenting"……..

On your first day in Art College you will be told that it is important to draw lots. You will be asked to draw lots for who is going to have an affair with a lecturer, who is going to have a nervous breakdown etc……

Another important thing to realize about Art school is that you can do anything you damn well like so long as you can justify it in long WORDS…NB. Art school slang has remained static since the 60's so speak like your parents O.K.?

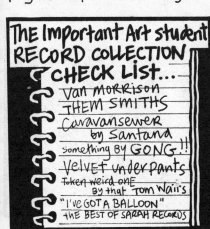

If you haven't got any of these essential ART SCHOOL type discs, we're afraid your first term's grant won't stretch very far……….

Another thing you'll have to do if you're a girlie is HAVE AN AFFAIR. You could choose the hippie who won't talk to anyone and has a mysterious gap in his history between leaving school and starting college

OR A LECTURER! Fiona has had an affair with a lecturer. She has come top in painting and sculpture and etching and silk-screen printing… NOTE THE PITFALLS OF THIS APPROACH……….

THE END!

GREAT POP THINGS → THE ROXY MUSIC STORY: ART GOES POP-CRAZY!! BY Colin Beno & Chuck La Mort

Byran Ferry was a coalminer in Durham like his father and his father before his father before that. But he, somehow, did not, as it were, "fit in", being as how he was obsessed with various ARTY things..................

Soon Byran plucked up courage to tell his dad and his dad and his dad before that Coal-mining was not for him. He wanted to go to Art School and combine Art and Pop like Andy Warhol did with Coke bottles.

Byran decided he would go to the Royal College of Art, so he could learn all about art and how to speak posh at the same time. He recruited the rest of ROXY MUSIC by putting up a notice in the ROYAL COLLEGE canteen.

Soon ROXY MUSIC became the "thinking man's SWEET" and got famouser and famouser. However, trouble was a-brewing in the ROXY "camp", as synth-player "BRAIN" Eno's popularity grew due to his fantastic lack of musical ability.....

Soon Byran got rid of "BRAIN" ENO for not knowing nothing about music, getting all the girlies, and going "PZARRP ZZZZ SWOOSH" during the quiet bits. But Mr Ferry was still unhappy as none of the girlies on the LP covers would snog him.

Byran then started making "solo" albums consisting entirely of songs written by other people. This was in stark contrast to the ROXY MUSIC LPs where he wrote all the songs. He was therefore more famous as a member of "ROXY" than he was as himself.

Ironically, Byran was no longer insanely jealous of ENO, he was now incredibly jealous of himself. HE split Roxy music up and embarked on a solo career and when this did not work he split himself up and reformed ROXY MUSIC. And so on.

After this had gone on for quite a while, Byran himself began to get confused and accidentally chucked himself out of ROXY music but finally met a girlie who would snog him and lived happily ever after. THE END.

GREAT POP THINGS → The Maniac STREET-PREACHERS "THE MOST ORIGINAL GROUP SINCE THE CLASH!!!" By Colwyn Ap Morton and Chuck whatever the Welsh for death is...

In 1991, as luck would have it, disaster struck. People's band The Clash, who previously championed revolution with their trousers with words on, "sold out" in a T.V. advert for trousers without words on..............

"But who will lead us?" cried the hip cred kids on the street. A new force was needed, young vibrant with skinny bottoms. Hailing from Blackwood, Gwent, the Maniac Street Preachers were the logical choice.................

So uncompromising was the band's fundamentalist Punk rock stance, that they languished in obscurity for the entire 1980's, turning down lucrative gigging opportunities and going shopping for their mums instead.........

The Manics practised really hard everyday at Pen-Y-Lan pond, a well-known local watering hole and secret meeting place of "THE DEAD HIPPY SOCIETY"......NEXT WEEK the Manics hit the BIG CITY (Newport, Gwent) and tour abroad (LONDON, ENGLAND)..............

GREAT POP THINGS → The ALARM Maniac STREET PREACHERS STORY Part 2: "Sponsored Suicide" by Colin Boredom & Chuck Dead Boys

The Manics took up where the Clash left off, wearing SHIRTS WITH WORDS ON (as a wry comment on the lack of words on the new trousers sported by the self-styled CLASH) to the total apathy of "squaresville, gwent".....

There are unconfirmed rumours that the Manics, like Dave Bowie and Sooiuixsie and her Hasbeens before them, flirted with the Nazis in the early part of their career. For whatever reason, they were shown the door by reactionary local promoters who were not ready for "punk"...............

So the Manics trundled across the Severn Bridge on their way to seek fame and fortune in London, England with it's red buses, conservative-voters and hip-groovy manchester scratty music scene......................

Soon the Manics had "made it big" like Iggy Pop and spawned hordes of imitators such as THE NEWPORT DOLLS & THE GLAM ORGANS. The papers dubbed them "The Welsh Clash" dye to a fleeting superficial resemblance to early punk.

THE END

Born Bob Zimmerman in Davenport, Missouri, the youthful Bobby Dylan was a leather-jacketed urban-style rock 'n' rolling rebel amongst folky ruralism. Until one day, Bobby was involved in a horrifying cycling accident.....................

Changing his name to avoid confusion with the famous Welsh poet Dylan Zimmerman, Bobby pulled up roots and took them to New York City, where he sold them and used the money to purchase one of those acoustical guitars.........

In Greenwich Village, Dylan stood out as a folky ruralist midst leather-jacketed urban rock 'n' rolling rebels. There were others (Phil Ochs, Woodie Allen, Burl & Charles Ives), but Bobby was exceptional because his symbolic lyrics allowed people to read their own meanings in...

But then he had a cycling accident and released his ironically-titled electric "Freewheelin'" album.....all the other folkies said he had sold out and just wanted to sell records and have hordes of starlets trying to snog him!....(TO BE CONTINUED)

GREAT POP THINGS → BOBBY DYLAN: Part 2

The first date of Dylan's notorious tour backed by the ironically-titled backing band THE BAND was in Newport, Gwent, Wales, England. From this originates the folky tradition of sticking one finger in your ear, just in case Bobby should "turn up"...................

Famous at the time were Bobby's "press conferences" where journalists would ask him questions and he would come up with witty pithy replies which were subsequently anal-ised by DYLANAPOLOGISTS who would bore everyone about him on the stairs at parties.............

About this time various new DYLANS were thrown up. These were usually discovered feeling sorry for themselves on the stairs at parties and signed by get-rich-quick records e.g. the famous Scottish folk-singer BOBBY DONOVAN.....................

This meant that anybody feeling a bit sorry for themselves could go into a record company with an acoustical guitar and make records about it, then get really rich, take loads of drugs, snog other pop stars, get depressed and make more records about it.....(TO BE CONTINUED)

HE TRIED TO CHANGE THE WORLD BUT ACTUALLY CHANGED HIS RELIGION AND HIS BACKING GROUP QUITE A LOT"

Bobby carried on making lots of records which nobody really took much notice of except his fans, the so-called DYLANAPOLOGISTS who would go through Bobby's garbage with bizarre, fetishistic vigour.........

A cycling accident caused him to team up with Alan Ginseng to make the motion picture "RENALDO AND THE LOAF" which had the Dylanapologists glued to their seats, whilst no one else has ever seen it at all, so the above panel is blank with pregnant symbolism (or pregnant with blank symbolism)

In the mid-70's and up to the present-day period Bobby, had a series of cycling accidents which caused him to change his religion and his trousers quite a lot. His Christian period produced the epic "God gave Names To All the Animals"......................

His Zen Buddhist period produced "ME & BOBBY McGHEE" with its "Nothing don't cost nothing 'cos it's free" refrain. Ultimately disillusioned he produced TOO MUCH OF NOTHING which told of his disenchantment with Zen Buddhism. Later he joined the NOTHING HILLBILLIES with Tommy Petty. THE END

GREAT POP THINGS → THE ADAM ANT story → "HE TRIED TO CHANGE THE WORLD BY DRESSING UP AS AN ANT!!" By COLIN B. morton and CHUCK DEATH

GO AWAY I DON'T LIKE ANY OF YOU, MAAAN!!!

Stuart and his Stick-insects? Peter and his Pismires?

DESTROY

When Punk started up, young Stuart Goddard's trousers were caught on fire with NEW WAVE FRENZY, and he frequented the fleshpots of SOHO to catch a glimpse of the SEX PISTOLS with their fantastic teenage philosophy of fun and music............

WE SHOULD LIVE LIKE ANTS LIKE IT SAYS IN THIS BOOK

CONSIDER HER WAYS
John Wyndham

He then went and formed ADAM and his ANTS. They put forth the proposition that human beings were a decadent lot and would be better off living like Ants under the ground milking little aphids and so forth etc. etc.............

YA BOO SUCKS ADAM! PUNK IS ESSENTIALLY A NON-CONFORMIST PHILOSOPHY...

IN THE TRADITION OF THE DADAISTS' SITUATIONISTS' AND OTHER NON-CONFORMIST PHILOSOPHIES...

WITH MORE SWEARING!

QUEEN MUM GAWD LUV 'ER

He was not popular with other punk-rockers who wore ridiculous outfits, didn't have proper jobs and said beastly things about the Royal Family, (who also wore ridiculous clothes and didn't have proper jobs etc. etc.).............

LEMME GET THIS STRAIGHT, YOU WANNA DRESS UP AS ANTS? BUT YOU'LL LOOK RIDICULOUS

PLANET GONG

Besides this, he had a difficult time persuading major record companies that "ANT music" was a viable commercial proposition. A well-known record company exec. is now known, to his undying shame, as "THE MAN WHO TURNED DOWN THE ANTS". (to be continued)

ADAM ANT Part 2: Incorporating the BOW WOW WOW story "DOG EAT DOG !!!"

adam you are not wanted here hint please leave so I can invent a group with annabella who is more sexy than you LU WIN

Adam decided to take hints from ex-PISTOLS manager Malcolm McDowell, who played a BEASTLY, caddish trick, throwing Adam out for being "Not sexy enough", replacing him with a girlie he'd discovered in a laundry basket, and forming BOWOWOW..............

Voices of tiny fans

HOORAY HOORAY HOORAY HOORAY

Taking the hint, Adam joined up with guitarist Marco Polo and formed another "ANTS"! He attracted a new generation of fans, the Antettes, who were fantastic 10-year-old girlies with shavedy-bits on the sides of their heads who lived for ADAM.....

YOU'RE NOT GOING OUT DRESSED LIKE THAT ARE YOU?

ADAM + HIS ANTS

Much to their mums' disapproval, the Antettes copied his uniform of foliage and leaves stuck in his hair for camouflage, and a white stripe across his nose that nobody knows what it has to do with ANTS............

Dear Sir,
I enclose photo of my teenage 10-year old daughter. She has become infatuated with some Pop Star...what shall I do?

Worried, Gwent

AUNTIE KAREN SAYS.....
Don't worry, she will grow out of it and shed her wings after mating, possibly becoming the Queen of a highly organized social colony!

Acme ANT COSTUMES made a fortune, whilst young boys ridiculed the 10-year-old girlies for dressing up as ants, do the ANTDANCE, and generally carrying-on-like-hymenopterous-insects about the place............

ADAM AND THE ANTS → PART THREE "THE TWILIGHT YEARS" by Col x Chuk

Most Antettes did, in fact, grow out of dressing up as ants and there are now only a very few twenty-something-year-old girlies dressing up as Ants in the "halls" of academia..................

His old anarcho-punk-rock fans thought he had "sold-out" and wrote letters which said things like "WHY OH WHY HAS ADAM ANT DESERTED HIS LOYAL PUNK FOLLOWING MERELY TO PANDER TO THE WHIMS OF 10 YEAR OLD GIRLIES WITH SHAVEDY-BITS ON THE SIDES OF THEIR HEADS?...WE TURN INSTEAD TO CRASS, CULTURE SHOCK AND VEGETABLE SACRIFICE...!"

Adam became an object of ridicule throughout the legs and breath of the UK., as comedians came up with fantastic jokes like "How many ears has Adam Ant got?" which doesn't really work if you write it down.............

But now; ADAM IS BACK! So dust off your ant costumes girlies and get ANT-Dancing again.....MOVE #1, put your right foot in...Move #2, left hand above the head...move #3, right hand above the head...move #4, cross your hands... move #5, left foot in etc.etc. THE END.

GREAT POP THINGS → The PAUL WELLER STORY: Part ONE.

THE JAM STORY / THEY TRIED TO CHANGE THE WORLD BY TELLING PEOPLE TO VOTE CONSERVATIVE! BY COLIN B. MORTON and CHUCK DEATH

Panel 1: Yes, you'll need some of them guitars wot you plug in the wall, some of that trendy gear from Carnaby Street and a name like the CREAM or the marmalade type thing....

One day in the mid-70's Paul Weller felt an adolescent urge. He got so tired of having sleepless nights that he went and told his DAD he wanted to form a group. His Dad, "Mr Weller", knew a bit about groups 'having seen "READY STEADY GO" once or twice during the 60's......

Panel 2: NO BRUCE, 'THE PRESERVE' IS NOT SNAPPY ENOUGH... The Pickle?

I LIKE THE QUEEN '84 / I ♥ LONDON

So Paul's Dad went and bought them loads of gear like what he had said and they started practising in Paul's Bedroom. Heeding his Dad's advice about group-names Paul christened them **The JAM.**

Panel 3: HELLO...THIS IS CALLED ALL NIGHT NONSTOP DANCING AND YOU CAN PONGO TO IT !!

PEOPLE TRY TO PUT US DOWN FOR OUR ALLNIGHT NONSTOP PONGO DANCING!

BOING!! FOOK SHOT / YES TONY WONVKIN'S SHALL WE SLAG THEM OFF OR SAY WE LIKE THEM? HMM JULIE SWEETNESS THIS BAND SEEM TO HAVE FOUND A CORRELATION BETWEEN THE DISCONTENT OF PUNKS + THAT OF MODS

They managed to get proper gigs in a pub called the SPOTTED COW. As they all had short hair, like Paul's Dad remembered off the telly, they were mistaken for an idiosyncratic "PUNK" band (as punk was just starting.) They soon adapted to this........

Panel 4: THIS IS ONE OF OUR OWN SONGS.... IN THE CITY PEOPLE TRY TO PUT US DOWN AND THEY SAY WE HAVE NO RIGHT TO GET AROUND....

isn't there an inherent contradiction in reviving an anti-nostalgic movement? / shut up you git / the press don't understand it! / THE QUEEN IS NICE / I'VE BEEN TO LONDON ZOO / I'VE BEEN ON A BIG RED BUS / WELCOME TO CARNABY ST.

Soon the Jam were being compared to "the" early "WHO" even though Paul had never heard of them and was only following his Dad's advice. Soon a revival of "MOD" (a sixties anti-nostalgic youth movement) started up! NEXT WEEK: what Paul DID NEXT!

PAUL WELLER Part 2: "The Atom Bomb is a Paper Tiger!" PAUL GETS POLITICAL !!!!!

Panel 1: ...support whatever the enemy opposes and oppose whatever the enemy supports it sez here...... VOTE TORY KIDS !!!

MAO'S LITTLE RED BOOK

With the increased success of the JAM, Paul began to think deeply about politics. Noticing that the then Labour government was run largely by middle-aged "squares" in suits which had NO STYLE, Paul turned to the works of China's CHAIRMAN MAO for advice...

Panel 2: DO YOU BITTERLY REGRET YOUR INSTRUCTION TO THE YOUTH OF THIS COUNTRY TO VOTE FOR THE RUNNING DOGS OF CAPITALISM IN 1979? YEH WE WOZ REALLY YOUNG & NAIVE AT THE TIME, I BITTERLY REGRET IT....ANYWAY WHY DO YOU ALWAYS MENTION THEM IN INTERVIEWS?

WHAT, THE TORIES Y'MEAN? NO, I MEAN DOGS Paul → Top Journalist

So popular were the Jam at the time, that "MODS" having just reached the age of consent and fired by Weller's advice were responsible for the 1979 Tory Election victory. Then Thatcher altered all the boundaries and the "CONS" have ruled ever since......

Panel 3: THE FACE FORWARD WITH FASHION

THE FINAL STRAW THAT BROKE THE CAMEL'S BACK BY THE CLIFF OF "MOD"

PAUL WELLER EXPLAINS WHY HE SPLIT UP THE JAM BY BOBBY HELMET

HE SITS THERE NONCHALANTLY STUBBING OUT HIS SOBRANIE IN HIS CAPPUCINO. THE SLIGHT RIP IN THE KNEE OF HIS JEANS SPEAKS VOLUMES. SO CASUAL AND YET SOMEHOW SO RIGHT. THIS IS PAUL WELLER, THE BARD OF WOKING, METHODICALLY HE TUGS THE COLLAR OF HIS OFF WHITE TRENCH COAT AS IF TO SAY " I AM ". THE WORLD LAY AT HIS FEET HE HAD TAKEN THE 3-PIECE AS FAR AS IT COULD GO, HENDRIX, CREAM, THE THREE DEGREES LAY SMOULDERING IN HIS WAKE LIKE SO MANY COFFEE DRENCHED SOGGY CIGS...WHY OH WHY, DID HE etc.

Paul was by now getting frustrated with the limitations of the 3-piece line up. So he got rid of the bass player who 'looked like he was crying and the bloke on drums with silly shades and formed the STYLE COUNCIL. What a great name for a band!..

Panel 4: HERE'S ANOTHER ONE ABOUT THE GENWUL STWIKE !!!!

The Style Council, consisting of Paul and FAB organist Milton Parker, became known as the CHAZ 'n' DAVE of Socialism, sang in French, got LEE P. LEE in on backing vocals & toured the UK supporting lisping left wing comedian WED REG and his labour party! T'END

THE JESUS AND MARY CHAIN STORY "They tried to change the world with their leather pants"

Identical twins Craig and Charlie Reid were born in Perth in the Outer Hebrides. For the first 27 years of their lives they stayed in their bedroom eating lots of sweeties and listening to pop records......

Eventually their mum told them she had run out of money for sweeties, and they would have to go and get jobs. Not liking the sound of this very much, they ran off to LONDON to seek fame and fortune.............

Naming themselves "THE JESUS AND MARY CHAIN" as a comment on how religion is commercialised like a supermarket or something, they soon found themselves bottom of the bill at a then-fashionable BOSSA-NOVA concert......

As luck would have it their was a RIOT and the Police were called. The boys made front-page in the tabloids and the NEW MYSRABLE EXPRESS whose journalists had got fed up with the BOSSA-NOVA craze they'd invented 2 weeks earlier...

"THEY TRIED TO CHANGE THE WORLD WITH THEIR FEEDBACK AND FUNNY HAIRCUTS"

As they were now the most controversial group to emerge from the BOSSA-NOVA craze of the early 80's, the J.A.M.C. advertised for a bassist and drummer in the back pages of MUSIC MONITOR (the pop weekly for the children of the middle classes)

Soon it was time for the J.A.M.C. to go into the studio to record their first single. As they didn't play their guitars at all but just stood around while they made feedback noises, the engineer, Paul Glitter, was a bit confused...........

The J.A.M.C. were now the darlings of pop intellectuals everywhere! Whereas punk rockers had played their instruments badly, Craig and Charlie didn't play at all! thus taking things a stage further out! But trouble was a-brewin'!

A radio one D.J. thought their record was about DRUGS, whereas it was about a girlie who wouldn't talk to the twins 'cos they wouldn't go to the pictures with her. But despite this (AND THE DRUMMER DANNY GILLESPIE GOING OFF TO FORM SPINAL SCREAM) the J.A.M.C. are still going today. THE END

GREAT POP THINGS → IN THE STUDIO WITH SINEAD O'CONNOR

BY COLIN B. MORTON & CHUCK DEATH

GREAT POP THINGS → The SECRET ORIGIN of THEM COCKATOO TWINS

BY COLIN B. MORTON AND CHUCK DEATH

One day, little Elizabeth Frazier was sent shopping by her mum. As she was an exceptionally good little girl she was allowed some sweets.

When she arrived at the spanking new shopping centre, Elizabeth was very excited to see a funny little notice..........

Lizzie hot-footed it straight to the old barn where she found Robin and Hector Cockatoo trying out some new things with an echo box and guitars....

Having no lyrics Liz thought quickly and pulled out her shopping list and sang that. They asked her to join and a fab pop act was born. THE END

ELVIN COSTELLO THE FAR FROM MELLOW FELLOW Part One "ELVIS C, he's MADE AN LP!"

Elvin Costello's real name is Decal Mc-Manus, he is the son of Mick Mcmanus the notorious TV wrestler. As a child in Liverpool Decal was often caught skiving off his "wrestling lesson" in order to play acoustical guitar in Folkie clubs.......................

So Decal and his dad decided on a compromise.. His dad would let him give up wrestling for singing, pro-vided he would sing vitriolic songs with a real guitar instead of having a toy guitar and singing about sai-lors, as previously had been going on...

He took the name Elvis Costello as a tribute to his two heroes Lou Costello a chubby comedian and Elvin Presley a rotund pop star. He hoped somehow to combine the singing ability of one and the wit and grace of the other in his new persona.....................

Elv got his big break during the "pub-rock" revolution of the mid-'70s when he appeared on the Bull Grumpy pro-gramme and told all the viewers at home that he spent the million pounds advance from stiffy records "Dahn the boozer"!!....

ELVIN Costello Part 2 "He tried to change the world with his GRUMPINESS!"

In the ensuing months to come, Elv shocked the sober world of rock showbiz with his oft controversial behaviour. E.G. with his savage jibe at acoustical-guitar playing folkie Steve Stills.....................

So spectacularly popular was Elv in the late '70s/early '80s that a generation of 'singer/songwriters that were, (ahem) "influenced" by Elv began to emerge. These sounded like Elv but didn't look like him.......

To combat this trend, Elv took to making loads of records not under his real alias but under differ-ent ones e.g. Napoleon 14th, Gil-bert O'Sullivan, Paul and Linda McCartney, Jilted John...... (etc.)

Notorious as a curmudgeonly type in interviews, Elv frequently ran foul of journalists, but he still main-tains a loyal following despite this cantankerousness and extraordinary hairy image............ (THE END)

GREAT POP THINGS → The IRON MAIDEN story: "THEY TRIED TO CHANGE THE FACE OF HEAVY METAL WITH THEIR SOCIALLY-AWARE LYRICS AND MONSTERS!" BY Colin B. Morton and Chuck Death

Iron Maiden were formed in the East End of London in 1977, at the height of "punk-rock" with it's attendant nihilism and funny clothes.....times were hard for "THE IRONS" as they were known to their 300-strong road crew and dozen or so fans.................

Being dedicated to Heavy Metal, the IRONS decided to "stick it out." Their luck turned when a journalist invented the NEW WAVE OF BRITISH HEAVY METAL, or NWOBHM as it was known for short, even though it wasn't much shorter.....

Meanwhile, in another part of the forest, young Dicky Tickerson was being expelled from St. Chadbourne's public school for general HEAVY-METAL-goings-on in the lower 4th dorm after lights out.................

Unable to find a "responsible" job like the army or the stock exchange, young Dicky went through several up and coming HEAVY METAL bands. Being an all-round sophisticate, however, he kept on not fitting in.......(TO BE CONTINUED.)

IRON MAIDEN Part 2: "my name is Dickie Tickerson, I'm caught between two stools, I'm too smart FOR HEAVY METAL, TOO rough FOR PUBLIC SCHOOL"

As fate would have it, "THE IRONS" were looking to get out of the rut that they, their monsters and 300-strong road-crew had found themselves in. So they placed an ad in "MUSIC MONITOR", the pop weekly for ex-public schoolboys.............

When Dicky turned up for the audition, he soon impressed with his sophisticated lyrics plus a solid Heavy Metal background in the likes of "SATAN'S MOTORPSYCHO MEATCLEAVERS", "DEAD HAMSTER", "JEZEBEL KRIST", "S.S. SPANDEX", "the Cancer Bunnies" etc.

So Dickie joined the IRONS and they never looked back, which was just as well seeing as they had a load of monsters following them about. Rock critics were impressed by the sudden leap into all-round sophistication which the IRONS' lyrics had taken.......

Iron Maiden soon made a huge commercial impact with their top socially aware lyrics which dealt with subjects and issues the kids on the street could identify with like, werewolves, vampires, monsters etc. etc. (TO BE CONTINUED)

GREAT POP THINGS → The IRON MAIDENS story PART 3, IN WHICH THE IRONS KNOCK OUT! CLIFF RICHARD ON TOP OF THE POPS! BY Colin B. Morton and CHUCK DEATH.

AND LURVE'S DONE GONE DOWWWNNN TO NUMBER TWO AND HATE GOT THE UPPER HAND.... YES IT'S NUMBER ONE IRON MAIDEN WITH SEND YOUR DAUGHTER TO THE SLAUGHTER MRS. WORTHINGTON

Last week as you recall THE IRONS recruited Dicky Tickerson and became a huge enormous HM. band. This paid off dividends in the early 90's when they recorded Noel Coward's "send your daughter to the slaughter mrs. Robinson" from THE GRADUATE...

SEND YOUR DAUGHTER TO THE SLAUGHTER MRS. ROBINSON, JUDAS LOVES YOU MORE THAN YOU WOULD KNOW, GOO GOO GA JOOB, MY BROTHER'S GOT A headache!

Also Dicky Tickerson got the top of the pops in the book chart with his highly acclaimed novel, "the story of Lord Cliffy Boooo....." here Mr. morton's writing tails off suddenly so I'd better carry on on my own. er....chuck here....um I've done a nice picture of the IRONS on T.O.T.P. but I don't know what writing goes here and I can't find Colin anywhere....

Oh speaking of headaches, I've got a headache now...quite a BAD ONE ACTUALLY.... I wonder where COLIN's GOT TO? I'M alone here and WHAT's that THUMPING NOISE on the landing?....

....Hello?.....

ningh yog so

HA·HAHAHAA!
HA·HAHAA!

THE END?

FANTASTICAL GRAND FINALE.........

Dave Bowie's XMAS panto
CINDERELLA
by Bertold Brecht!

SCREENPLAY: COLIN B. MORTON, AUDIO/VISUAL REALISATION, MAKE UP AND THONGS: CHUCK DEATH

Ye Cast:

Cinderella .... Dave Bowie (himself!)
Buttons Pop .... IGGY!
Ye Ugly Sisters .... BONNIE LANDFROG, BROS, MORRISSEY, ELDRITCH, BONGO FROM U2 etc.
THE PRINCE .... Prince
Fairy Godmother .... GARETH NUMAN
The Prince's Flunkies .... The London Boys, George Clinton
plus SHEENA EASTON, WENDY JAMES and Frank Sidebottom AS "THE PUMPKIN"

COME ON CINDERELLA, SWEEP UP ALL THIS BROKEN GLASS....

YES SISTER LANDFROG SOB SOB

POP

Once upon a time there lived a fantastic girlie called **CINDERELLA** ('cos she lived among the cinders). She lived with her ugly sisters who were very ugly and her best pal "Buttons". He was called "Buttons" because his buttons kept popping off........

I WONDER IF I'LL GET A SNOG OFF THE PRINCE, SISTER SPIGGY!

SOME HOPE SISTER MOZZETTE! HE WON'T GET NEAR ENOUGH WITH THAT HUMUNGOUS CHIN OF YOURS!!!! YOURS!!.. YOURS!..

When she heard that the PRINCE was holding one of his enormous Balls, she sat on a stool and cried whilst her ugly sisters tried on lots of fantastically over the top party dresses and fantasized about snogging His Majesty...............

OH I AM SO SAD I CANNOT GO TO THE BALL

CRASH!

FEAR NOT CINDERELLA THE PRINCE SHALL CRAVE YOUR SUGAR WALLS!

That night as Cinderella sat alone crying, there was a tremendous **CRASH!** as a light aircraft came hurtling down the chimney.... It was her Fairy Godmother, who wanted to know why she was crying and was such an essentially passive character......

I'll change this pumpkin to a car, that you might go so VERY FAR, I'll change your RAGS to clothes so GLAM, the Prince your BODY WILL want to Jam!!

see OINK #20

The Fairy Godmother promised to use various magics to enable Cinderella to go to the Ball, thus reinforcing the myth that working-class people cannot alone unshackle the chains of their oppression but must rely on the intervention of external forces...........

So at last Cinderella could go to the ball, and join in her stepsisters' contest to have their identities defined by association with a rich and famous majestic purple sort of person (Is this getting too Brechtian & un-festive? Yes? good)............

The Fairy Godmother warned Cinderella that she had to leave the Ball before the stroke of midnight or her fine GLAM-ROCK clothes would fall to bits and her fairy Batmobile would, amazingly, turn back into a humble paper maché pumpkin.........

When she finally arrived at the Palace, she stood out because of her fantastic glam-rock clothes and radiant beauty. The ugly sisters did not recognise her, but were insanely jealous.... But this did not bother Cinders as she only had eyes for the PRINCE!

It came as no surprise to everyone when the Prince asked Cinderella to dance, such is the sexism and sentimentality inherent in fairytales like this. Cinders, thoughtfully removed her high heels so the PRINCE would not seem so ridiculously short.........

Cinderella was so busy "boogie"-ing on down with the Prince that she lost all track of time... at the stroke of twelve she remembered what her Fairy Godmother had told her, and ran from the Palace just as her glam-rock clothes started falling to bits!

The Prince was really cheesed off because he wanted to snog Cinders and make a stageshow and video out of it and hadn't had a failure like this since Susannah Hoffs out of the Bangles. Fortunately one of his entourage found the glass Platform slippers Cinders had left behind and had not disintegrated due to a logical flaw in this fairytale......

Although this seems a fairly arbitrary way to allocate power and privilege, the Prince and his energetic disco-dancing flunkies went off and scoured the land in search of the lovely Cinderella so she could become Mrs. Prince etc. etc................

So Cinderella tried on the GLASS PLATFORM slippers and they fitted! Well I never, a surprise ending, yet! So they got married, strengthened the ties of monopoly capitalism, reinforced sexist values and lived happily ever after........ **THE END.**

"In the start when they begun
ROCK AND ROLL were very young
it's very sad but now I'm told....."

GREAT POP THINGS → ROCK AND ROLL ARE VERY OLD! Help the Aged "BUY OUR SINGLE!" BY COLIN B. MORTON and CHUCK DEATH

Do you want my body
Do you know
I'm 60?

Darling... you smell horrible tonight!...

OH NO! NOT THE....

LOCK UP YOUR GRANDmothers "joke"......

er, sorry

We salute the fantastic inventor of Rock'n'Roll mr Bill Haley, the only Rock'n'Roll star to die of natural causes and a jolly round chappie to boot...............

We salute Rod "the Mod" stewart, the cuddly wrinklie who still surrounds himself with blonde and leggy debs despite his advancing years...............

We salute Eric "Derek" clapton who flirted with Punk & changed with the times to stay at the top during <u>the</u> and <u>his</u> nineties.......................

We salute them ROLLING STONES who've just signed to VIRGIN RECORDS for loads of dosh and plan to spend their retirement touring outer space.....THE END

"Rock'n'Roll once stood for sex
But now it's stars are ancient wrecks
and ROCK is King from Pole to Pole
But no one knows what happened to ROLL"

that's all folks